The Dog Comes With The Practice

Expanded 2nd Edition

The Dog Comes With The Practice

Tales of a Junior Doctor in Ireland and Canada

by

Tom Baskett

Expanded 2nd Edition

Clinical Press Ltd.
Bristol UK

© Tom Baskett 2023

The right of Tom Baskett to be identified as the author and artist of this work has been asserted by him in accordance with the Copyright, Designs and Patents Act 1988.
All rights reserved. No part of this publication may be reproduced, stored in a retrieval system, or transmitted in any form or by any means, electronic, mechanical, photocopying, recording or otherwise, without prior permission from the copyright owner.
While the advice and information in this book is believed to be true and accurate at the time of going to press, neither the author, the editor, nor the publisher can accept legal responsibility for any errors of omissions that may be made. The publisher makes no warranty, express or implied, with respect to the material contained herein. Case histories and names have been altered to preserve confidentiality.
First published in collected form in the UK 2020, expanded 2nd edition 2023.

A catalogue record for this book is available from the British Library.

978-1-85457-118-2
The Dog Comes With The Practice
Expanded 2nd edition
Tom Baskett

Cover design: © Mark Goddard 2023

Published by:
Clinical Press Ltd.
Redland Green Farm, Redland, Bristol, BS6 7HF

For Yvette

TABLE OF CONTENTS

- Acknowledgments *8*
- Introduction. *9*

Chapters
1. Futterly. *11*
2. OK, Baskett, You Start in Casualty. *17*
3. It's Not Your Fault, Doctor. *22*
4. Damage Control. *26*
5. Sunday Morning Bible Class. *29*
6. All Hell Broke Loose. *31*
7. Sunday Evening Coming Down. *36*
8. Von Wrecking Houseman's Disease. *39*
9. The Wards. *42*
10. Sudden Death Becomes Cardiac Arrest. *48*
11. You Could Have Fooled Me. *53*
12. Wetting the Bed. *57*
13. "Peace Comes Dropping Slow." *61*
14. "Though Wise Men at Their End Know Dark is Right." *67*
15. General Practice 101. *72*
16. The Dog Comes with the Practice. **77**
17. In the Name of the Father. *84*
18. Never Again, Doctor. *88*
19. Just Getting a Few Things for the Children's Supper. *93*
20. A Criminal Offence. *101*
21. The Firing Squad. *106*
22. Fetal Distress. *111*
23. She's Having a Fit. *116*
24. Beyond Futterly. *121*
25. The Pope Rules. *125*
26. Up North. *133*
27. He's a Lovely Man. *137*
28. She's Still Bleeding. *141*
29. Arctic Family Planning. *146*
30. Seventh Son. *149*
31. Polar Bear Alert. *152*
32. The Sign of the Bloody Feet. *154*
33. Surgery by Phone. *159*
34. Sleep Well, Samantha. *163*
35. The Ethics of Life. *166*
36. Sister McCormick. *171*
- Bibliography. *176*

Acknowledgements

A large thank you to my old friend Patrick Taylor. We met at medical school and, for a time, were roommates at the Queen's Elms Hall of Residence. We both ended up doing obstetrics and gynaecology in Canada: he in Calgary and Vancouver and me in Winnipeg and Halifax.

Taylor always had literary tendencies and, after he retired from clinical practice, became a best-selling author with his *Irish Country Doctor* series of fifteen books, chronicling the mythical exploits of an Ulster GP – one Doctor Fingal Flahertie O'Reilly.

In 2020 he rested his quill and kindly agreed to keep me on the editorial straight and narrow with my own literary effort, and has done so for both editions of this book. My writing is based on the look, rhythm and sound of words; but Taylor actually knows the rules of writing and he agreed to guide my syntax, grammar and punctuation. After I had looked up the meaning of syntax, I readily accepted his generous offer – hoping that some of his publishing success might rub off.

He has done his best to correct my work, but I may have snuck a few errors past his editorial gaze. He has pointed out numerous misplaced modifiers and my tendency to bursts of pronoun confusion. Although I don't see why one shouldn't be allowed the occasional split infinitive, even if I accept that one's participles should never dangle.

I am grateful to Dorothy Tinman for her helpful non-medical perspective and review of the manuscript.

Kate Connon, Doreen Martin and Sylvia Nelis, Royal nurses from the 1960s, kindly shared details of their time as student nurses. Thanks to my classmate and friend, Manton Mills, for his reminiscences of Doctor Frank Pantridge and to Lisa Marie MacPhee for her expert restoration of the photographs.

My biggest thank you goes to my wife, Yvette, who typed the manuscript, as she has for all my books. She encouraged me to put these stories down on paper, and has lived through all of it with me. Everything I do is with her in mind.

Introduction

This collection of stories describes some of my more memorable and formative medical encounters as a junior doctor in Northern Ireland and during my early years in Canada. They are written as they happened, but in some instances the details and location have been modified to avoid potential identification. Others represent an amalgam of cases.

The names of individuals have been changed, except for the following: Professor John Henry Biggart, Dean of Medicine, the Queen's University of Belfast (QUB); Dr. Graham Bull, Professor of Medicine, QUB; Brigadier Davidson, Medical Superintendent, Royal Victoria Hospital (RVH), Belfast; Dr. Frank Pantridge, Consultant Cardiologist, RVH; Dr. John Geddes, Senior House Officer to Dr. Frank Pantridge; Dr. Jack Hildes, Director, Northern Medical Unit, University of Manitoba; Dr. Jean McFarlane, Consultant Obstetrician, Winnipeg General Hospital (WGH); Dr. Mervyn Roulston, Head of Obstetrics and Gynaecology, (WGH); Dr. Patrick Taylor, classmate; and Cissie, our cleaner in the Huts.

Every patient and all other characters not listed above have been given fictitious names.

How can I be sure my memory is accurate from fifty years ago? Well, I keep everything: old exam papers, receipts, letters, all the case reports from my student days and the thirty case studies that formed the thesis required to sit the membership exam of the Royal College of Obstetricians and Gynaecologists. I can, for example, tell you that my litigation defence insurance annual fee was £3 in the late 1960s, and that I bought a new pair of rugby boots for £3 10s in 1965. I have kept notes on cases of interest, and through the years have told these stories many times to myself, long-suffering family members and friends; eyes raised to the ceiling – 'He's off, reminiscing again.' I have, I think, largely avoided embellishment distortion – although I can't be certain that some may have crept in. Obviously, the dialogue is not verbatim, but it was along the lines I have written.

This expanded second edition adds ten new chapters and represents an historical record of medicine in the 1960s and early 1970s. It therefore describes the limitations, and in some cases the strengths, of medical practice more than fifty years ago.

There are a number of stories I cannot tell. They were of extremely rare circumstances and, even if slightly modified, might be recognised. Such cases bring to mind the quaint old Ulster saying: "I would not of had of believed it, if I would not of had of been there."

For me these stories represent some of my most precious and privileged encounters – both funny and sad. As such, they reflect my schooling in medicine and in life. Here they are.

T.F.Baskett
Halifax, Nova Scotia

Chapter 1
Futterly

You don't get to be a doctor without going through a lot of examinations and answering repeated skill-testing questions. In theory this is to reassure the public that you can respond with knowledge and aplomb to any medical misdemeanour that might befall the tax-paying citizenry. In truth, many of the exams did nothing of the sort, but they had to be overcome while you tried to learn how to be a doctor.

My career with examinations started at age eleven and continued in serious mode for the next twenty years. The life-defining exam in the United Kingdom (UK) of the 1950s was the eleven-plus, taken, as the name suggests, at the age of eleven. Successful candidates were admitted to a grammar school, which might ultimately lead to university. I missed sitting the eleven-plus because we were living in Washington DC, where my father worked as Agricultural Attaché at the British Embassy from 1950 to 1952. So, between the ages of nine and eleven I was subjected to the very different American education system, with much less discipline. The teacher was kind and called me 'honey', as opposed to, 'Be quiet, Baskett, small boys should be seen and not heard,' and six across the palm of the hand with a ruler for more serious transgressions.

We returned to Northern Ireland in September 1952, just as the school year was beginning. I was fortunate to be accepted at Belfast Royal Academy, because of my sojourn in the United States and the fact that my two older brothers had been at the school. The difference in my previous two year's education was profound and it took me some time to readjust and catch up. I had become used to the American decimal money system; so much easier than the UK pounds, shillings and pence; with twenty shillings in a pound, twelve pennies in a shilling and halfpennies thrown in for good measure.

I slowly recovered, but not without some pretty spectacular failing marks. I tied for last place, with eleven percent, in the first Christmas term exam in Arithmetic. The results of exams were read out before the whole class. We had one maths teacher who announced poor results as, 'Failed utterly, Baskett, failed utterly – eleven percent.' He was known to us as

'Futterly,' and I had quite a few futterlys over the years. Luckily, we hadn't heard of self-esteem or post-traumatic stress disorder, so those of us in the low mark category were able to cope.

I was consistently poor at Maths, and therefore also poor at Physics – both were a constant struggle for me. Consider the following question:

A man with one leg shorter than the other, such that his left leg stride length is 2 feet 8 1/2 inches and his right leg stride length 3 feet 1 inch, is walking up a 12-degree incline 100 yards long. Given that each degree of incline shortens his stride length by 0.45 percent, how many steps would it take him to cover the 100 yards? Calculate the number of additional steps it would take if he faced a 9 mile-per-hour wind, assuming that each mile-per-hour decreases his stride length by 0.3 per cent. Discuss the mathematical principles involved in your calculations.

OK, I've embellished this a bit, but this is the sort of rubbish we had to put up with. Which begs the universal questions: 'So what?' and 'Who cares?' (Many years later, when I was an examiner for the Royal College of Physicians and Surgeons of Canada, I brought this 'So what?' and 'Who cares?' principle to our exam committee. We applied it to all the multiple-choice questions submitted for our specialty examination.)

I slowly rose in the academic ratings at school from futterly, to mediocre, to the occasional pass. By the time the province-wide junior certificate examination came along (age 15 years) I managed to pass. One key part of this was Latin in which we had to get a credit, fifty-five per cent or higher, in order to do law or medicine at university. I got fifty-six per cent – the first sign of a tendency to overachieve.

I have to admit that my main focus was to represent the school at rugby football and athletics (track and field) – both of which I achieved. I liked English and History and, while I didn't excel, I passed. In my final year I had a good English teacher and began to like poetry. The only book I kept from school was my green, dog-eared copy of *A Pageant of English Verse*, which I still have. I enjoyed Keats, Milton, Wordsworth, Yeats, and the sonnets of Shakespeare – Willie the Shake, as we called him.

I did advanced sciences in my last two years, which led to another futterly low point in the Christmas term physics exam of my final year at school. Once again, I came in equal last with eleven per cent, but rebounded six months later with a stunning forty-one per cent (forty per cent was the pass mark) – overachieving again.

In the final provincial schools' senior certificate exam, I just scraped through in Physics and Maths, but did well in Biology and Chemistry – sufficient, to my great surprise, that I had enough credit to apply to study medicine at the Queen's University of Belfast. I had expected to do another year at school.

The final hurdle for admission to study medicine was an interview with the all-powerful Dean of Medicine, John Henry Biggart. Thus, polished from head to toe, and wearing my school rugby colours tie, I showed up for my interview. I knew my academic record was weak, but I did meet the minimum requirements. My older brother, Peter, had just finished and passed his final medical exams, and in those days having a family precedent in the faculty was a plus. My interview was short.

"I see from your tie that you played rugby for your school, Baskett."

"Yes, sir."

"Do you intend to play rugby at Queen's?"

"Yes, sir."

"Good, we'll look forward to seeing you in October."

And that was it, my focus on rugby at school had paid off – and I wasn't even that good. I know, any modern reader is wondering, 'How on earth did this buffoon get into medical school?' Well, that's how.

Accordingly, in October 1958, I presented my seventeen-year-old enthusiastic self, along with about 100 others, to start medical school at Queen's. Six years later, fifty-nine of us (thirty percent women) would emerge with our medical degrees. The first year was really just preparation: Botany, Chemistry, Zoology and, the dreaded Physics. There were written and practical exams in all of these; representative questions from these exam papers, follow:

Botany. *'Describe the structure and origins of wood.'*
Chemistry. *'Discuss the thermal decomposition of urea.'*
Physics. *'Give an account of the thermionic emissions of electrons.'*
Zoology. *'Give an account of the development of a frog.'*

Gripping stuff, no marks were given, just pass or fail – fine by me.

The next big hurdle was in the middle of third year after five terms of Anatomy, Embryology, Physiology and Biochemistry. This was a monster exam and, although a resit was allowed, by the end of third year about forty per cent of our class had failed or dropped out. The rest of us went up to hospital for the last three and a half years. The penultimate exam was Final

Part One in fifth year: Pathology, Pharmacology, Therapeutics, Microbiology, Forensic Medicine and Social Medicine (Public Health). There were quite a lot of failures, but resits were allowed, and most who got this far would ultimately prevail and qualify.

Those who pushed the limits, and took the maximum allowable number of resit examinations, were said to have taken the 'long course'. One particularly good athlete was allowed three years to pass first year, because he represented the country at the Commonwealth Games. He went on to take the maximum number of resits at every examination, and ended up qualifying after eleven years.

Finals, at the end of our six years, was quite an ordeal spread out over three weeks. The failure rate was ten to fifteen per cent. The first week was three-hour essay exams in all the major clinical subjects. The next two weeks were taken up by major and minor clinical cases and oral exams. The major clinical cases were critical, and a poor performance in any of these could mean failure in the whole exam. You were assigned a patient on the ward and had thirty minutes to take a history and do a physical examination. Two examiners joined you, one from outside Northern Ireland, and to them you presented the history and clinical findings. You were asked to demonstrate the physical signs, upon which great emphasis was placed in those days of limited diagnostic imaging techniques. This was followed by a detailed oral exam on the diagnosis and treatment of the patient.

The patients were all told about the exams and how important they were to the students, who, if they passed, would become doctors. One assigned patient took this so seriously that he refused to give the student any of his medical history. "I don't want to help any substandard student become a doctor," he said, "if he can't find out what's wrong with me, he shouldn't be allowed to pass." The student was assigned another more realistic patient.

All the teaching hospitals in Belfast were geared up for these exams, where it was known as 'Finals fortnight'. The finale came on the last Friday evening when the examiners had their decisive meeting at the university. This meeting was held in a room under the cloisters that surrounded the university quadrangle. Sometime after six in the evening the Dean, a man who loved tradition and ceremony, appeared in his academic gown with a sheet of paper in his hand. He walked slowly across the lawn to the middle of the quadrangle. From beneath the surrounding cloisters most members of the class and a few other observers, some sent to get the result for a candidate who couldn't bear the drama, moved out towards the Dean. As the crowd steadied around him, he began to read the class list in alphabetical order: "Aitken, pass, Anderson, fail, Barnes, pass," …. and so on down the whole class list.

For those of us who passed it was a massive relief, but also awkward because of a friend or two who failed. Either way, it was followed by a night of alcohol consumption that provided a serious challenge to the resilience of our liver enzymes.

Tom Baskett outside the Huts at the Royal Victoria Hospital in May 1964 - one month before qualifying as a doctor

Chapter 2
OK, Baskett, You Start in Casualty

"OK, Baskett, you start in Casualty," said the Brigadier. It was eight a.m. on the first of August, 1964 and twenty-six newly minted doctors, eight women and eighteen men, were gathered in the old surgical extern lecture theatre just off the main corridor of the Royal Victoria Hospital, Belfast. We had spent the last six years together as medical students at the Queen's University of Belfast, passed our final exams in June, and were now about to be unleashed as the first line of defence against the medical woes of any Belfast citizen unfortunate enough to need treatment at the Royal.

The Brig, as he was known, was also a Queen's medical graduate and had a career in the regular army, retiring as a brigadier general. After army service, he became the medical superintendent of the Royal and was responsible for the distribution of the resident medical officers (known as 'housemen') – the most junior of the junior doctors. The women resident medical officers also referred to themselves as 'housemen.' The entire day-to-day medical administration of the hospital was covered by the Brig and his office secretary. Likewise, the whole of nursing and housekeeping administration fell to the Matron, her secretary and her assistant matrons. There were no lay administrators. In each ward or unit the senior consultant was medically responsible and the sister (head nurse) oversaw nursing standards. (The title ' Sister', was not a religious order, but retained from the era of the earliest hospitals, where patients were cared for by Catholic nuns.) Everyone knew who was in charge. Compare this to the vast and almost impenetrable matrix of modern hospital administration.

We were to live in the hospital permanently for the next twelve months – either in the 'huts,' or the east wing. The 'huts' was, in fact, a single Nissen-style hut situated between the mortuary and the tennis courts. It was sometimes called 'Mortuary Mansions.' It had twenty rooms off a central corridor, ten for live-in medical students and ten for housemen. Each room was very basic, eight feet by eight feet, with a washbasin in one corner and a phone on the wall above the head of the bed. It was an all-male enclave; the females lived in the east wing. As housemen we had our own dining room and sitting room, also in the east wing and just off the main hospital corridor. I lived in the huts, looking out on the tennis courts. I was very familiar with the huts as I had spent about eighteen months living there as a medical student.

The Royal was the main teaching hospital in Belfast with about 700 beds. In addition, housemen covered a number of satellite units: ENT, plastic surgery, and a chest hospital. The backbone of the Royal was the main 400ft long corridor off which, on one side, the twenty main medical and surgical wards were situated side-by-side. Adjacent to one end of the corridor were the gynaecology, neurology and neurosurgical wards and at the other end, the endocrinology and dermatology wards. Off the other side of the corridor were the east and west wings, and the Casualty department. The west wing housed the Matron's offices and student nurse accommodation. With the exception of the endocrinology and dermatology wards, all of the clinical units were on the same level.

At the top of the medical hierarchy were specialist consultants, supported by a broad-based pyramid of junior medical staff, houseman (intern), senior house officer (SHO, junior resident), registrar and senior registrar (senior residents). Although designated as junior medical staff, senior registrars were often ten to fifteen years after medical graduation and had many postgraduate qualifications. In some situations, patients were better off in the hands of a senior registrar than a consultant.

I cannot remember much about the Brig's introductory message. We were to be paid £30 a month ($84.00), plus free accommodation, food and laundry. Each rotation was for three months – six months surgical and six months internal medicine. There was no real orientation as such, we were supposed to know the ropes from our time as students, and to some extent this was true. I believe there was a consultant appointed to Casualty, but I never knew who it was and never saw him (it would have been a him) in my three months there. Casualty was at that time the designation in the United Kingdom for what would later be called the Accident and Emergency (A&E) department. In North America it is the Emergency Department.

Thus prepared, the four of us who were appointed to start in casualty turned up at nine a.m. ready for work, or so we thought.

The main part of Casualty was the Ambulance Room with seven

curtained-off cubicles, each containing a full-length trolley, known to our North American colleagues as a gurney. At the end of this room was the ambulance entrance, through which the more serious stretcher-borne cases arrived. In one corner was sister's tiny office and on the opposite wall was an illuminated box for viewing X-rays. The other end of the ambulance room opened onto the large waiting area and off to the right were Rooms A and B for the walking wounded – small cubicles with a chair. On the other side of the waiting area were a small surgical theatre (operating room), a suture room, a septic theatre for infected wounds and a three-bedded ward for overnight observation. This was to be our domain for the next three months.

We had three working shifts: day, nine a.m. to six p.m. (two to three doctors); the short night, six p.m. to midnight (one doctor) and the long night, six p.m. to nine a.m. (one doctor). It worked out at eighty to ninety hours a week.

Throughout the hospital the key personnel were sister and the senior nurses. I learned as a student that they were the backbone of the hospital and not to be too proud to ask for their help. Woe to any young doctor who tried to come the heavy with an, 'I'm the doctor and I'm in charge' approach.

It was all done very diplomatically, as in:

"Sister, I've got a patient here with this, this and that – what do we usually do?"

To which Sister would reply:

"Well Doctor, we usually do that, that and this."

"I can do that and that, could you please arrange for this?"

"Certainly, Doctor."

The nurses of the 1960s were at the end of the Florence Nightingale era of military-style discipline and training. The ranks were clear and inviolable: Senior Sister with bright red uniform, Junior Sister with navy blue and staff and student nurses in a striking royal blue. All ranks had white starched collars, cuffs and aprons. Staff nurses and above wore the white starched 'fall' – the triangular head-dress that framed their hair and face. Student nurses had a smaller cap and a different coloured badge for first (green), second (blue) and third year (red). Everyone knew who was who, and where they stood. They looked incredibly smart and efficient; patients could not help but feel better in the presence of a 'Royal nurse.'

Another vital member of the Casualty staff was Sam, the porter. His main job was to wheel patients over to the Radiology department (pre-ultrasound), wait while they had their X-ray and bring them back. From nine a.m. to five p.m. there was a radiologist who read the X-ray and sent a written report back with Sam. Over the years Sam had stood behind the radiologist on hundreds of occasions while he read the film. Thus, he had become quite expert in a limited but casualty-relevant portion of radiology. After five p.m. we were on our own and had to read our own X-rays. On evenings, when Sam returned with the film, the following was a typical encounter:

Doctor and Sam stand in front of illuminated X-ray in ambulance room.
"Well, Sam, what do you think?"
"I was wondering about that rib on the right, Doctor."
"You think the sixth rib is fractured just there."
"Seventh rib, yes, Doctor, right there."
"I think you're right, Sam, I don't see anything else, do you?"
"No, Doctor, I think that's it."
"Just a bit of strapping then."
"Yes, that's what they usually do, Doctor."

Now, lest you think we were completely clueless, we did get better, and in fact quite good as our experience grew. In the beginning, however, it was important to seek and accept advice from those in the know.

Our medical back-up was the registrar (resident) in each of the specialties: internal medicine, surgery, gynaecology, neurosurgery and orthopaedics. In a sense as housemen we performed triage, dealt with what we could, and then referred to the appropriate registrar. In my three months I never saw a consultant of any specialty in Casualty.

It could be intermittently gruelling, Friday and Saturday nights were the worst, mainly due to drunks and car accidents – often one and the same. It was the pre-seatbelt era. There was no gun violence, mostly fights with blunt trauma and bottle slashes. We did a lot of suturing. Unsupervised, we put on plaster casts at night – in our inexperienced hands some casts were so heavy that they not only splinted the broken bone of the affected limb, but almost immobilised the whole patient.

Otherwise, it was the usual spectrum of acute medicine and surgery: heart attacks, heart failure, acute asthmatic attacks, pneumonia, diabetic comas, strokes, acute abdominal emergencies (appendicitis, perforated duodenal ulcer, bowel obstruction), trauma, fractures, and haemorrhage from various orifices. Apart from children and obstetrics, which went to their respective hospitals on adjacent sites, anything bad that could happen to the human body came to us.

It was, in a Dickensian sense, 'the best of times and the worst of times,' some of these are recorded in other chapters. For me it was the best way to begin life as a doctor; after that they couldn't scare me anymore – at least not with acute emergencies. It was a good start.

Chapter 3

It's Not Your Fault Doctor

After two weeks in Casualty, I was beginning to get the hang of things – until one morning when I didn't have the hang of things at all. It was a grey day with a light rain falling as the ambulance men brought in the body of a young man on their stretcher. He was from east Belfast and they had picked him up just outside the shipyards where he worked. He had been cycling to work when he was struck by a bus; perhaps his bicycle wheels had slipped on the wet cobblestone street. When the ambulance arrived, he had some signs of life, so they brought him straight to Casualty at the Royal. (In the 1960s the ambulance service was mostly a fetch-and-deliver service, in contrast to the modern highly equipped and trained paramedics).

When I examined him, it was only to confirm and certify his death. His body appeared unmarked and, lying on his back, he just looked as though he was asleep. The back of his head, however, was caved in and his neck was probably broken. Sister helped me and we found his name and address from his union card; the only identification in his pocket. His name was James Wilson. A policeman at the accident had followed the ambulance to hospital, so we asked him to go to the address and inform Mr. Wilson's wife. Sister emphasised that he was only to tell her that her husband had been in an accident and that he was at the Royal. She gave the policeman her own office number for the wife to call.

Mrs. Jane Wilson had two children under the age of four and, when she phoned, sister had to convince her that it was serious enough for her to come to the hospital at once. Fortunately, the policeman had stayed with her while she phoned from the local shop and he gave her a ride to Casualty in his car.

In the meantime, I got on with seeing other members of the ailing public. About an hour later sister came to me and said Mrs. Wilson was in one of the rooms outside the minor surgical theatre.

"I have told her that her husband's accident was serious, but I'm afraid it's up to you as the doctor on duty to give her the details. I'm sorry Doctor, but I'll be with you."

I went into the stark, white-tiled room where sister had set up two chairs beside a small table, upon which rested a cup of tea. In any part of the hospital, in any type of crisis, a cup of tea was always an early response.

Jane Wilson sat in one chair and looked up as I came in. Her pretty face, framed in brown hair, was pale and tense – and clearly prepared for bad news. Sister introduced me.

"Mrs. Wilson, this is Doctor Baskett, who was on duty when your husband was brought in by the ambulance this morning."

I sat down beside her.

"Mrs. Wilson, I am very sorry to have to tell you that your husband died as a result of the accident this morning."

"Oh, God …. Oh, God …. Not my Jimmy …. I just saw him off to work," she started sobbing.

"I'm terribly sorry, I know it's a horrible shock for you."

"Are you sure, Doctor? …. Are you sure …? What happened? …. He can't be dead."

"There was an accident with a bus …. A collision when he was on his bicycle…. He must have hit his head on the cobblestone road…. He would have been unconscious immediately …. He wouldn't have suffered at all."

I was so choked I could hardly speak and what I was saying seemed so inadequate. But I was a doctor now and I was supposed to be able to do this.

We sat for a while. Then I took her hand and asked, "Would you like to see him?"

"Can I? …. Should I? …. Yes, I would."

Sister had Jimmy Wilson's body lying on the trolley in the adjacent theatre. His head wound was cleaned of blood and a towel and pillow were skilfully placed. On his back he looked perfect. We stood on each side of his body.

"Oh, Jimmy …. Oh, my Jimmy" she said quietly, over and over, as she held his hand and then gently placed her head on his chest. Tears were rolling down her cheeks, and mine. It was such an intense and profound expression of grief that it was quite overwhelming.

I went around the head of the trolley and as she stood up, I put my arm around her and said, "I'm sorry," again and again. I couldn't think of anything else to do, as I desperately tried to control my own distress.

Sister came from the corner of the room and rescued me. She took over by enfolding Mrs. Wilson in her arms. "Thank you, Doctor, I can take it from here," she said gently, "I think you are needed in Room A."

Room A was where the minor, walking cases were seen. Sister had arranged that I would be assigned to this easier role while I regained some composure.

I went to the first cubicle, took the chart from the clip outside, pulled back the curtain and said, "Well now Mr. Watson, what can I do for you?" …….. "It's my back doctor." The dreaded acute back strain, for which we could do little but prescribe pain killers and rest. Most of these patients were looking for a sick note to cover a few days off work. I was happy to go through the mindless routine. Then, thankfully, I had two cases with minor lacerations that needed suturing; concentrating on a technical task is the best possible therapy when you are upset or very tired. I liked the surgical side of medicine, so suturing was a pleasure for me.

As I walked back from the suture room across the waiting area, I saw the back of Mrs. Wilson as she left alone through the doors of the main entrance to casualty. She was such a forlorn figure that I felt there must be more we could do for her, but I couldn't think what.

I found Sister in her little office, with the ubiquitous cup of tea.

"How are you, Tom," she said

"I'm fine."

"Liar," she said kindly

"I'm afraid I wasn't very good with Mrs. Wilson. I really didn't know what to do."

"It's never easy," Sister said. "But you were kind and she could see that, and kindness is the most important thing in our business. You explained what happened to her husband and showed you cared enough to be upset and that's all anyone can expect of us. You have to remember, it's not your fault Doctor, you can't fix everything."

"How was she going to get home?"

"I ordered a taxi and gave her the fare. I have a small fund for these occasions."

"I think I should ring her GP and warn him."

"Good idea" she said. "I'll get him on the phone."

I had advanced with Sister from 'Doctor' to 'Tom'. This was no small thing in the 1960s, when formality of address was pretty strictly observed in hospital.

Luckily her general practitioner was in and I told him the situation.

"Do you know her well?" I asked. He was silent for several seconds.

"Know her, I delivered her 23 years ago – one of my first home deliveries. I have been her GP all her life. I'll drop round to her house this afternoon. She'll need help, but she's a very sound young woman, a real trooper and she'll cope. Thanks for letting me know."

For some reason this case affected me more profoundly than anything I had ever encountered before. Even now, more than 50 years on, I still occasionally wake up at three a.m. thinking about it. I can still see her face collapsed with grief. Perhaps it was the fact that she was the same age as me, or the loss of a young life in the blink of an eye, or the thought of her returning home alone and trying to explain to a two and a three-and-a-half-year-old why their dad wasn't home from work, and the sight of her leaving the hospital and walking out into the rain alone.

Even though I had experienced a lot on the wards as a live-in medical student I was completely unprepared for this. Most of the deaths on the hospital wards were expected and involved older people with serious disease. At no point in our six years as students had we any training in death and dying or breaking bad news – absolutely zero. There was no quiet room where one could talk privately to bereaved family members. Sister had improvised as best she could.

As my career unfolded, I had to break bad news more often. I probably got better at it, but I was never able to hide completely my own feelings. This is not necessarily a bad thing; as long as you're not a blubbering idiot I think patients appreciate that you, to some extent, share their distress. Things are done much better now; medical and nursing students have specific teaching in death and dying and in breaking bad news. Although I still think there is a place for the cup of tea.

Chapter 4

Damage Control

This is the only story in this collection that is not from my time. Rather, it was from the era of my late brother, Peter, who was a houseman at the Royal in 1958-59, six years before me. The event became legendary and, perhaps somewhat embellished, was passed down through the years. Here it is, as I remember it from my brother.

As Peter told it, in the late 1950s the porter in Casualty was John, no surname, he was just always known as John. He was ex-army and had risen to the rank of sergeant. John was very strong and built like the proverbial brick outhouse. He was extremely loyal to those he served – the doctors and nurses in Casualty. His presence and strength were helpful on Friday and Saturday nights when we often had to deal with belligerent drunks.

Late one Friday evening Gerry Lowry was brought in by ambulance after fighting in a bar. He had sustained a number of lacerations to his head and face. The ambulance driver reported that they found him lying on the floor of the pub, drunk but conscious.

Lowry was a big burly man, who worked as a builder. After admission to Casualty, he was seen by the houseman, Roger Wilson, who sutured the lacerations. However, one large and deep laceration on top of Lowry's head worried the houseman. Although he was able to stop the bleeding and suture the wound, Wilson felt there could also be a fracture of the skull bone. If so, there could potentially be underlying bleeding around the brain. Therefore, he ordered an X-ray of the skull. By now, Gerry Lowry had been in Casualty for about two hours, had partially sobered-up and was demanding to be allowed to leave. Doctor Wilson was very firm and told him he must have his skull X-rayed first, and why it was important – enter John.

"John, this man must have his skull X-ray. Under no circumstances is he to leave the hospital until I have seen it and cleared him to go. This is very important. I think he may have a skull fracture."

"Right you are, Doctor Wilson," said John.

John positioned Gerry Lowry firmly in a wheelchair and trundled him across the waiting area to the Radiology department. While there, John was relieved by another porter and went to the hospital cafeteria for his supper break. In the meantime, the skull X-ray film was taken, and the patient returned to Casualty. Roger Wilson read the film and found no fracture. He re-examined Mr. Lowry and pronounced him fit for discharge.

Gerry Lowry left Casualty, but instead of turning right to the exit doors he turned left through similar doors that led onto the corridor that ran along the entrances to the wards. Returning from the cafeteria, along that same corridor, John spied his former charge and remembered the clear and urgent instruction from Doctor Wilson – 'Under no circumstances is he to leave the hospital until ….' John, thinking Lowry had done a runner, confronted him.

"Now then, Mister Lowry, you come along with me back to the doctor."

"I've just feckin' well been discharged," said Gerry Lowry, full of righteous indignation.

John could see no difference between Lowry's righteous indignation and his former belligerence. A mighty tussle ensued between two strong men – both with right on their side. Eventually John prevailed, dragged Lowry back to Casualty and, rather like a faithful Labrador retriever, dropped him in a crumpled heap at the feet of Doctor Wilson. As well as some additional bruising Gerry Lowry now had a broken right forearm.

"Bugger," said Roger Wilson, "we're really in the manure now."

To make matters worse Lowry's brother, having been alerted that Gerry was in Casualty at the Royal, was on the phone. The staff nurse had to tell him that, yes, Gerry Lowry was still in Casualty having his injuries treated. The brother was on his way.

Understandably, Gerry Lowry's righteous indignation reached new heights, along with serious litigation threats. While his broken arm was treated with a plaster cast, a damage-control plan was formulated.

John quickly acquired a number of high-profile injuries. His left forearm was put in a plaster cast and a sling. Blood, not hard to find in Casualty on a Friday night, was soaked into bandages and applied to his right hand, along with a particularly impressive one around his head. He was a pathetic sight and instructed to sit still, not to speak, but to give the occasional groan.

This, then, was the scene when Gerry Lowry's brother arrived at about one in the morning. Gerry recounted the shameful treatment he had received and that his arm had been broken by a member of the hospital staff. Threats of litigation and media-interviews rose to new levels.

Doctor Wilson made soothing noises and acknowledged that there had been a misunderstanding resulting in a physical encounter with a member of the hospital staff. Without rancour or judgement, he reminded them of the events leading to Mr. Lowry's admission to Casualty. His trump card was Exhibit A – pulling back the curtain to the cubicle on the slumped, battle-scared figure of John, who emitted a well-timed pitiful groan.

Roger Wilson delivered his final pitch: "We quite understand your ire and no one regrets this evening's events more than I. However, I have been on the phone with the hospital lawyer (pure bluff, as far as we knew there was no such person) and I am advised that any litigation will be met with a strong counter-suit. As his physician I can assure you our valued and vital porter has sustained far worse injuries than your brother – to which I am willing and qualified to attest."

The defence rested successfully. They don't teach that in medical school.

Chapter 5
Sunday Morning Bible Class

Every other Sunday morning at eleven a.m. an exclusive clinic at the Royal Victoria Hospital provided relief for men suffering from the long-term effects of gonorrhoea – it was known as the Sunday morning Bible class. The relief was in the form of dilatation (opening up) of a stricture (narrowing) of the urethra (the canal from the bladder through the penis). The stricture was the result of a gonorrhoeal infection acquired in the days before penicillin treatment.

There was no appointment necessary, the men knew when to show up. They came every few weeks when their stricture began to narrow, to the extent that they had difficulty producing a proper stream of urine to empty their bladder. There were between one and four challengers each Sunday. As live-in medical students this was one of our duties.

The key was to make sure there was adequate local anaesthesia. Using sterile gloves and a syringe (without needle) full of local anaesthetic gel one filled the urethra with as much gel as possible. It was important to allow at least five minutes for the local to take effect.

The dilators looked quite formidable – metal, about ten inches long and curved at one end. There were multiple dilators of various diameters in a set. The patients usually knew what size 'worked for them', so it was wise to listen to their guidance:

"They usually start with a fourteen and work up to a twenty-one, Doctor."

They knew we were students but often gave us the honorary 'doctor.' First names were not used in those days.

The most important part of the procedure was the manoeuvre to get the curved tip of the dilator around the base of the urethra as it angled through the prostate and into the bladder. It really was a case of 'right hand down a bit' at the correct point. Occasionally, the hand of the patient would come up on top of yours to guide the proper angle – these were seasoned campaigners. Legend had it that the first man in the queue came out to the waiting area after his dilatation and either gave a thumbs up or down to his fellow sufferers. If it was a thumbs down the others left and came back next week, hoping for a more skilled practitioner.

I lived in hospital a lot in my last two years as a student and took the bible class many times. I got to know some of the regulars, in fact they were all regulars. Many of them were veterans of World War One and had acquired their venereal disease in France. I remember one, William Craig, in particular. He was a small spare man in his seventies, about five feet, four inches in height. His weathered face was topped with a few wisps of white hair on a pale scalp. The pallor of the latter was due to the perpetual presence on his head of a 'duncher,' as the flat tweed cap was known. The duncher was ubiquitous and worn indoors and out by the workers of that era. In his own way he carried a quiet air of composure and dignity that was appealing.

William Craig was one of a dwindling number of survivors of the Ulster Division that fought so bravely at the Battle of the Somme in World War One. They were initially organised in 1913, as the Ulster Volunteer Force to retain the link of the North of Ireland to Britain – the unionists, opposed to Home Rule in Ireland. With the outbreak of World War One they were formed, almost 20,000 of them, into the 36th Ulster Division of the British Army. On the first of July, 1916, the start of the Somme offensive, the Ulster Division was the only one to take its objective. Unfortunately, the divisions on either side could not, leaving the Ulster troops open to fire from the front and both flanks. In a few hours there were 2000 dead out of a total 5,500 casualties. Four Ulstermen were awarded the Victoria Cross that day, the highest award for valour – three of which were posthumous.

Over a few visits we became comfortable with each other and would chat a bit. He had worked as a riveter in the shipyard and lived in the Protestant area of Belfast. Some of the finest ships built in its heyday by the big shipyard, Harland and Wolff, had rivets put in by Willie Craig. As an apprentice he would have worked on the *Titanic*. I once asked him about the Somme. He said he was there, but wouldn't be drawn – only to say, "We did our bit, it was pretty grim."

He was the only patient that morning and I watched him leave, limping on his arthritic hip, coat collar turned up, duncher in place as he walked out onto the Grosvenor Road. Who could know what epic events had been experienced by this inconspicuous looking wee man shuffling along the street in Belfast on a dismal grey Sunday morning?

There is a saying, which I admit I haven't always followed:

'Be kind to all people, everyone's fighting a battle.' Willie Craig had certainly seen his share of battle, but he wasn't ready to talk about it yet.

Chapter 6
All Hell Broke Loose

"Get your arse back down to casualty, Taylor, we're up to our necks in broken bodies here." My phone call to fellow casualty houseman, Patrick Taylor, was brief and urgent. I was on the short night (up to midnight), Taylor was on the long night (up to nine a.m. the next day). As it was fairly quiet in the late evening he had gone to our sitting room for a cup of tea and a cigarette, while I held the fort. As it turned out it was going to be a long night for all of us; the Divis Street riots were about to exact their toll.

The background to the Divis Street riots of September-October, 1964 was as follows. The United Kingdom (UK) general election was scheduled for the fifteenth of October, 1964. There were twelve seats in Northern Ireland (NI), one of which was in West Belfast - the district around our hospital. The local republican candidate (opposed to the union of Britain and NI) set up his election headquarters in a disused shop on Divis Street, a predominately Catholic area about a mile from the Royal. In the shop window he displayed the Irish tricolour flag (green, white, and gold), to signify his support for a united Ireland. This was in conflict with the Flags and Emblems Display Act of NI, which forbade the display of the Irish flag on the grounds that it could 'cause a breach of the peace.' It was doing nothing of the sort, but it did stimulate the extreme Protestant preacher and politician, Ian Paisley, to put sustained pressure on the NI government to remove the flag. The job of enforcement fell to the NI police force, the Royal Ulster Constabulary (RUC), the large majority of whom were Protestant.

The candidate refused to take down the flag, so the police forcibly removed it, the candidate replaced the flag, the police removed it again, and so on. This precipitated demonstrations by up to 1500 local and other citizens in and around Divis Street, which at times developed into violent confrontation with the police. It went on for four nights, two of which involved serious riots and led to many casualties.

It started about eleven in the evening on the last day of September. A police van pulled up outside casualty and the doors to the ambulance room were burst open by a tall, burly RUC sergeant. He was a man in his fifties with short grey hair showing at the edges of his cap.

"We need some help here, I've got six injured police in the van," he said.

The nurses and I pulled out the trolleys from the ambulance room cubicles, rolled them to the van and transferred the three most injured men back into the cubicles. The others were able to walk or limp in under their own steam.

"There's more to come," said the sergeant, whose name was George McAvoy.

Taylor and I got to work on the three stretcher cases. Sister came into my cubicle and said, "You need to come and see this one now." The urgent tone in her voice made me respond at once.

In the next cubicle I found Constable Billy Clark. He was, as they say, 'white as a sheet'. He had been hit by a missile of heavy metal grating that struck him on the left lower side of his rib cage and abdomen. He was in a lot of pain. His pulse was a rapid 110 and his blood pressure low at ninety over fifty. I raised the foot of his trolley to help combat this shock and put in an intravenous drip of saline solution. I also took a blood sample to ensure there would be two pints of compatible blood available for him should it be needed.

"Bit of a rough night, Constable," I said.

"Yes, Doctor, I didn't see it coming, so I wasn't braced for it."

"Any other injuries?" I asked.

"No, that one just flattened me. I found it hard to breathe. I can only breathe shallow or I get a sharp pain in my ribs, here," he said, indicating his left lower chest.

He had probably broken his ribs, but my main worry was potential damage to any internal organs - specifically the spleen, which lies under the rib cage on that side. The spleen, which is about the size of the fist of its owner, is part of the lymphatic-immune system. It is vulnerable to rupture and bleeding from an injury, such as that sustained by Billy Clark.

On examination his left lower rib cage was extremely tender to compression, consistent with one or more broken ribs. This could be confirmed later by X-ray, but for now I wanted to be sure he wasn't bleeding into his abdominal cavity from a ruptured spleen. If there was a significant amount of bleeding it might be detected by a sign called 'shifting dullness.' Fluid inside the abdominal cavity is dull to percussion by the examiner's fingers. If one rotates the patient's body from one side to the other, and there is free fluid inside, the area of percussive dullness shifts from side-to-side. [As medical students, one of our more ponderous and boring lecturers was known as Professor Shifting Dullness.]

While I was starting to carry out the test for shifting dullness, Constable Clark removed any doubt by collapsing on all clinical fronts. He groaned and lost consciousness, his pulse was weak and well over one hundred and his blood pressure had dropped to seventy over nothing.

"That's, it, Sister," I said. "He's definitely bleeding inside, we have to get him to theatre (operating room). You phone Wards 19 and 20 and tell them we're on our way. I'll get a nurse to help me push him there. Oh, and ask the lab to send the blood straight to the ward."

"Right," she said, as she poked her head around the curtain and shouted, "Nurse, come here now."

The surgical ward on take-in that night was 19 and 20. 'Take-in' meant they admitted and looked after all surgical emergencies for those twenty-four hours. Their surgical registrar (senior resident) would be in the hospital. Ward 20 had a large operating theatre attached.

I increased the rate of the saline intravenous infusion to flat out. The nurse and I pushed Constable Clark on his trolley out of the ambulance room, across the waiting hall and through the doors onto the long corridor that ran along the entrances to the wards. The casualty waiting area doors were opposite Ward 6, so it was almost one hundred yards to Ward 20, the last on the corridor. There may not be an Olympic event for the hundred-yard dash with constable-laden trolley, but if there was, the nurse and I would definitely have been medalists. We were, I thought, particularly impressive in our final cornering through the heavy plastic doors into the ward.

Luckily, Johnny Maxwell, an experienced senior surgical registrar was on duty that night, and was waiting just inside the entrance to the ward.

"Nice driving," he said, "Stirling Moss* would be proud of you."

"This is Constable Clark, I'm certain he's bleeding from a ruptured spleen," I gasped. "Two pints of blood should be on its way." As Maxwell checked him over, I filled him in on the clinical details while I regained my breath. "Bet you a pint it's his spleen," I said.

"I won't take your bet, but I'll buy you a pint for your trolley-pushing endeavours," he replied.

Stirling Moss (1929-2020) was the top British racing car driver of that era, and a household name in the UK.

"You're on."

"We'll get him done right away. You'd better get back. I hear things are warming up down there," he said, as he wheeled Constable Clark through the doors to theatre.

"Right, I'm off." I ran back to Casualty.

I was fortunate to have had time to get Billy Clark sorted out. As Sergeant McAvoy said, "There's more to come." How right he was, all hell broke loose—ambulances, police vans, and cars brought a horde of casualties over the next three hours.

It was all hands-on deck as we recruited other housemen and medical students. Sister managed to conjure up extra nurses from the wards or the nurses' residence. There was no disaster plan, or if there was, we were unaware of it – we just got on with it. From now on it was rapid triage, deal with what you could, and refer to the appropriate specialty registrars, who all pitched in.

Fortunately, most of the casualties were walking or hobbling wounded. The injuries were mostly blunt trauma. There were no guns or bombs involved. It was a spontaneous uprising and the weapons used were opportunistic: bricks, metal grilles or grating, and concrete pavement slabs broken into throwable-sized pieces. The most sophisticated was the petrol bomb: a milk or beer bottle partially filled with petrol (gasoline) with a rag stuffed into the bottle neck, which was lit and hurled at police and other vehicles. A bus and several police and civilian cars were burned and destroyed in this manner.

It was a lot of X-rays, fractured bones and plaster casts, bruises, bandages and slings, many sutured lacerations, some minor burns, and the occasional Constable Clark with trauma to the abdominal wall and possible injury to internal organs. In between the relatively minor trauma one had to be sure you were not missing a serious head injury – the neurosurgical registrar was kept busy. And, of course, the usual medical and surgical emergencies unrelated to the riot. There were not many of those that night, so I think they may have been diverted to other hospitals by the ambulance men.

The official count of injured policemen was forty-six, and the majority of these were on that last night in September. By six in the morning as we were tidying up, big Sergeant McAvoy was almost in tears at the carnage wrought on 'his men.' Certainly, that first night most of the casualties were police rather than civilians. There never was an official tally of how many civilians were injured.

The next night, the first of October, was the reverse. The police were more prepared and had better personal protective gear. The majority of casualties were civilians, with the same profile of injuries as the night before. There were police baton-inflicted wounds as well as injuries from the projectiles thrown by their fellow rioters. Sergeant McAvoy was back again and looking much happier, despite his second 'all-nighter.' "Better tally tonight, Doctor," he said to me; his relief at balancing the score was evident.

I felt sorry for the RUC who had to enforce an unnecessary ruling. For the injured civilians and local property owners it was also a disaster. The spark for the riots was such a trivial event and only allowed to ignite because of the persistent demands of one extremist politician. In retrospect, the whole episode was precipitated by the needless enforcement of a coercive political tantrum. The republican candidate who displayed the flag came last in the election.

The RUC came in for much criticism over the years as a biased pro-Protestant police force. I worked in close contact with them during my three months in casualty and found them to be decent and even-handed. We were especially grateful for their presence on Friday and Saturday nights, when the occasional belligerent drunk could make life difficult.

The Divis Street riots were, to some extent, a harbinger of the much more serious 'troubles' that started in 1969 and would last some thirty years. For us, as two-month-old doctors, it was a gruelling two days and nights, but it was also exciting, and we did some good. It was a chance to prove ourselves. We were young and resilient.

Chapter 7
Sunday Evening Coming Down

Sundays in 1960s Belfast were bleak, austere and generally grim. The dominant Protestant approach to the Sunday observance of no work and no play, was to shut down all commercial and recreational activity. All shops, pubs, restaurants, coffee/tea rooms etc. were closed. Public playgrounds were closed. This extended to locking the gates to these sites and, if children managed to climb over the surrounding fence, they found the swings and other mobile equipment were chained to render them unusable. Fun was definitely forbidden. Sundays were for church, homework, and improving oneself. Most people would not even cut the lawn or work in the garden.

The Catholics had the better of it. After attending mass there were community activities, including organised games - Gaelic football and hurley were played on Sunday afternoons.

As a result, Sundays in Casualty could be quiet – with a reduction in work-related accidents, drunk driving, and other trauma.

I was the lone doctor on duty in Casualty one Sunday evening, and things were quiet.

An elderly woman was in one of the small rooms for ambulant patients.

"I think she's just a bit depressed," said the nurse as she handed me the card of the patient, seventy-year-old, Mrs. Harding.

"Bloody hell," I thought, this is supposed to be a casualty department, not an open house for all and sundry with minor ailments. Wrong again, Baskett.

I pulled back the curtain to find Mrs. Harding sitting on the chair in the corner of the small cubicle. She was plainly but neatly dressed, with grey hair held in place by a head scarf.

"I'm terribly sorry to bother you Doctor, I know you must be busy, but I have to talk to someone. I think I might be going mad."

Something about her gentle, defeated demeanour lowered my raised hackles – I could sense a lost soul.

"How can I help you, Mrs. Harding? We're OK for time, things are quiet at the moment."

"I live alone since my husband died three months ago, but I keep hearing him. I know it's not possible, but I do. I hear him coughing."

It turned out that her husband of fifty years had recently died of lung cancer, after a lifetime of smoking. During the last six months of his life he had slept in a separate room so that his coughing would not disturb her sleep. Now she heard him coughing as she drifted off to sleep, or she might wake suddenly to the same sound.

I reassured her that she was not mad and that this was a normal part of her grief. I did not really know that, but it seemed likely. Even then, it seemed inappropriate for me, a third her age, to be advising a seventy-year-old about grief. I just couldn't find the right words, probably because they didn't exist – at least not to me. So, I asked her how she and her husband first met; I found that most people with long marriages liked to talk about that. They had met as teenagers at a church social event – a common way for youth of the opposite sex to get together in those days. They had no children. She talked for quite a time about their life together, and it was clear how much she loved and admired him. Once she got started, I just sat back and listened.

I really had nothing to offer her but sympathy and listening medicine. It was something I had not encountered before, like a lot of things since I started work as a doctor. We had no experience with grief counselling; in fact, I don't think it existed in the 1960s – at least not as a recognised entity.

I offered her a few sleeping pills, but she decided against them.

"In a way, I still like hearing him."

She said she felt better now she had a chance to talk about it. "I just felt overwhelmed today, I'll be alright now."

I wrote a letter and gave it to her to take to her GP.

"Make sure you go and see him. He will be able to help."

"I will Doctor, and thank you for your kindness, I feel much better."

*

I found cases in which you could do nothing specific to fix the patient's distress to be the most emotionally tiring. It was much easier to deal with a definitive medical problem, for which you could take precise action to alleviate or cure. Even minor ailments, providing you could fix them, could give great satisfaction – reflecting a surgical mentality, I suppose.

Working in casualty provided the two extremes: serious illness and trauma, as well as minor walk-in complaints. You were also witness to just about every emotion of which humans are capable. In that way it did provide valuable preparation for general medical practice.

(I did not connect it at the time, but in retrospect this case confirmed the truth of Shakespeare's lines from the play *Macbeth*: "Give sorrow words. The grief that does not speak whispers the o'er fraught heart and bids it break.")

Chapter 8
Von Wrecking Houseman's Disease

I got engaged to be married on the afternoon of the eighth of November 1964, the birthday of my wife-to-be. It was a Sunday and later that evening some of my friends in the huts arranged cover of our duty on the wards and got in a supply of drink. We ended up with a sort of stag party which got seriously out of hand. It was the first real drinking get-together we had since we started our houseman's year on the first of August. We roamed between several rooms, including mine. Late-on someone slipped and put his elbow through one of the many small panes of glass in the window of the room. He broke the glass but did not cut himself – result, roars of laughter all round, followed by other deliberate elbowing out of glass panes to sustained merriment. Various missiles, including chairs, were thrown in an unruly outburst of paediatric behaviour. The walls of the huts were made of soft fibreboard which could be punctured with a confident karate approach, provoking further jocularity. At the end of this relatively short, but exuberant burst of activity, several rooms, including mine, had considerable damage—mostly to the windows. A chair leg was impaled through the middle of the mirror on the wall above my wash basin, producing a not unattractive starburst effect. At about two in the morning there was a partial sobering-up and recognition that work would resume in the morning and we retired to bed.

I awoke to the sound of broken glass and other debris being brushed up the corridor outside my room. Cissie, our cleaner, was on the job. I swung my legs out of bed and straight into shoes to avoid the broken glass on the floor, steadied my hung-over body, and opened the door.

"Jeez, Cissie, I'm very sorry, I got engaged yesterday and we had a bit of a do last night. I'm afraid things got out of hand and we got a bit destructive. No excuses, it was just very bad behaviour. I'll help clear up the glass."

"Don't you worry, Tom. I'm glad to see it. Youse fellows have been at it night and day for the past three months without a break. You can't keep going like yous'ns have without letting off a bit of steam. It's long overdue."

Cissie was our cleaning lady who looked after the huts. She was a great wee woman from the local area. I had known her for the last three years when living in the huts as a medical student. She was in some ways the class psychologist, at least to those of us who came through the huts. I can remember her taking on one of my classmates who had given up and stopped studying before our final exams. Cissie went into his room and gave him a severe bollocking for quitting and got him back on track, where the rest of us had failed. She had known generations of students and housemen, many of whom were now consultants. She was a legend to us, and I suppose a bit of a mother figure. Certainly, we were 'her boys.'

"So, Tom, you finally got engaged to that dark-haired wee beauty of a nurse you've been going around with for years."

"Yes, I did, Cissie."

"Good for you. She has an unusual first name, hasn't she?"

"Yes, it's Yvette. There are no French connections in the family, but I think her parents just liked the name."

"What's her surname?"

"McCormick."

"Well, that's a solid Ulster name, so you're all right there. She's a sister now, isn't she?"

"Yes, she's theatre sister in gynaecology."

"Well, you certainly don't get to be a sister in the Royal unless you're pretty good. You two have been together a long time, so, you should be OK. I wish you both the very best, so I do."

"Thanks, Cissie. Bless your heart."

"Away on with you now. Get yourself dressed and back up to your ward. I'll clear up here and get the rest of these scallywags up and back on the job."

Forgiveness and the seal of approval from Cissie — so, all was right with the world.

Cissie was typical of the cleaning women throughout the hospital. Each ward had it's own domestic, under the supervision of sister. They were a vital and integral part of the ward staff, with a strong propensity for tea-making at the first sign of need. Every member of each ward or unit in the hospital, from consultant to cleaning lady to student knew who each was and their role in the system. At a time when no one talked of teamwork or used administrative jargon there was real teamwork and each of us knew we were part of that team. With more and more professional administrators having no role in direct patient care, there is much talk of teamwork and other uplifting administrative-speak, but little or no actual teamwork on the ground. The main complaint one hears from medical and nursing staff now is that they work in shifts assigned to different areas of the hospital, so that in many instances no coherent team exists.

After the wreckage in the huts, which was obvious with broken glass strewn on the tennis courts, we expected serious retribution from the hierarchy. We awaited a bollocking from the Brigadier or the Dean. Perhaps they would dock our pay, although there wasn't that much to dock. As it turned out nothing happened, it was never mentioned; perhaps they agreed with Cissie or they had done something similar in their time. Those of us with broken windows, however, were punished to the extent that the glass panes were not replaced until April. The fog and wind-driven rain came into my room, but I was not going to complain about this self-inflicted discomfort. I taped plastic sheets over the window, but it was still a cold winter and at night in bed I had to wear my rugby socks and a jersey to keep warm.

And the name Von Wrecking Houseman's disease? This was a take-off on Von Recklinghausen's disease, an obscure condition with skin discolouration and multiple small swellings along the nerves under the skin. At that time, it was considered important to know about eponyms - the name of the person who first described a disease, and Von Recklinghausen rolled nicely off the tongue. It came from my consultant, who greeted me at the morning ward round:

"Ah, Baskett, I understand you got engaged and precipitated a nasty case of Von Wrecking Houseman's disease in the huts." Much dutiful laughter from those assembled. He was pretty proud of his joke, so of course I agreed with him.

"Nice one, sir."

Chapter 9
The Wards

Housemen were assigned to a ward for three months. A ward was, in fact, a combination of two individual wards, one for women and one for men, linked by a space that served as a kitchen and nursing office. The wards were known by their number; wards 1 (women) and 2 (men), were known as 1 and 2, and so on down the corridor to 19 and 20. Each ward was long and open, with the Nightingale layout of ten or eleven beds along each side and one bed in the window bay at the end. There was a side ward with one or two beds. Thus, the total beds per ward was about twenty-five, and they were always full. So, the houseman was responsible, at his or her level of competence, for the care of fifty patients.

The medical staff included a senior and a junior consultant, a senior registrar or registrar (senior resident), a senior house officer (junior resident) and the houseman (intern). There were also two live-in medical students. The nursing staff was led by a senior and junior sister, along with one or two staff nurses and several student nurses.

During the day many of the houseman's duties were low-level and clerical. Along with your live-in students you wrote up all the patient's medical records, took all the blood samples, started the intravenous drips (IVs) and did any necessary procedures, such as pleural taps (drainage of fluid from outside the lungs) and lumbar punctures (insertion of a needle into the lower spine to collect fluid from around the spinal cord for analysis). There were no addressographs or pre-printed patient labels, so all laboratory and X-ray requisition forms were written out by hand, as was labelling of the blood sample tubes.

Until the end of my houseman's year the syringes and needles used for blood-sampling were not disposable. After use, you rinsed the glass syringes thoroughly and tested the needle by running it across your fingernail to ensure there was no barb. If there was, the needle had to be replaced. Once a day all syringes and needles were individually wrapped in gauze and placed in a perforated metal box which you took to the sterilisation department. These were returned in time for the next day's blood-taking.

Much of this work was delegated to the medical students. Nowadays, this would be regarded as a 'non-educational' experience – 'scut work' is the demeaning North American description. However, the benefit as a student was that you were seen by the patients and the ward staff as having a vital, albeit small, role in the overall work of the unit. You were therefore accepted on the ward and in pole position for all clinical learning encounters. In my final year as a medical student, I lived-in the whole time, in part because I had exceeded my eligibility to stay at the Queen's Elms university hall of residence, and had nowhere else to live.

The sickest patients were kept in the beds nearest the entrance to the ward – the nursing office end. As patients got better, they were moved down the ward to the end by the window bay. This was, in a sense, the convalescent end of the ward and the patients were well enough to chat back and forth and to exercise their Belfast wit. This end of the women's ward could be intimidating for a student or houseman on his round of blood-taking.

In the early 1960s there was an American television series, *Doctor Kildare*, that was popular in the United Kingdom. Doctor Kildare was a young handsome hospital doctor who always managed to save the day in each dramatic weekly episode. Among the recovering women patients on the ward there was usually a ring-leader, I'll call her Mrs. McNamee, who led the others in the occasional good-natured, jocular harassment of the students and housemen. As you approached that end of the ward with syringe and blood-collection tubes you might face the following:

Loud and exaggerated kissing noises ….

"Here comes, Doctor Kildare. Oh, Doctor, come quick, I've come over all weak, I need you now," result, peals of laughter from her ward mates. "Oh my God, it's not Doctor Kildare after all, it's Dracula and he's after my blood."

"Behave now, Mrs. McNamee," I said, "Or I may have to order some more blood tests to find the cause of your sudden weakness, and possibly get Nurse Boggs to give you one of her special high enemas."

"Don't you dare, Doctor, I don't need no enemy" ('enemy' was the local witticism for enema – and a good one at that.)

As I walked back up the ward, after collecting the blood samples, I overheard one of the other patients say: "Sure, our doctor's far better than Doctor Kildare, so he is." Some degree of acceptance, then, from the convalescent heckling gallery. It was time to get Mrs. McNamee and a few others discharged, they were far too well and troublesome to remain in hospital. Our female colleagues, of course, might have to run the same gauntlet on the men's ward.

The main collective event of the day was the morning ward round by the medical staff and sister. This entailed going around the ward and checking each patient. It could be quite intimidating with the full retinue of sister, the consultant, all junior medical staff, and medical students. As a junior you presented the case of each patient whom you had admitted. Not all consultants did a daily round, in which case it was taken by the senior registrar or registrar.

It was at these rounds that bedside teaching occurred – the backbone of our clinical education. This usually involved many skill-testing questions for the juniors. Some of the consultants were showmen, they were almost all men, and could be entertaining. One such was Frank Pantridge, the cardiologist, whom I have mentioned in other chapters. Frankie P, as he was known to us, but never to him, had a well-developed Ulster sense of humour and a particularly biting line of repartee.

In the 1960s there was still a lot of rheumatic heart disease in the local population. Diagnosis of the effect this had on the valves of the heart and their function was made by listening with the stethoscope. The acquisition of this clinical skill was essential and, as juniors, we spent time seeking patients with this disorder to gain the necessary experience. Frankie P tested this aspect of the student's ability on his ward rounds.

If you missed the diagnosis he might say: "Sister, please arrange for this student to have an audiogram" (hearing test). Or he could respond to an incorrect answer by taking your stethoscope, checking it over carefully, and handing it back to you with the comment. "The problem lies between your ears, not with your stethoscope." If your answer was really bad, he would declare, "Please tell me you are a student from the Faculty of Engineering who has wandered in here by mistake."

In the modern humourless educational milieu this type of banter would be considered demeaning to the student and would not be tolerated. Perhaps we were less sensitive, but we didn't feel belittled by his humorous critique. Indeed, Frankie P did accept a degree (a limited degree) of back-and-forth banter in this vein. On one occasion we managed to sabotage a particularly annoying, pushy and hyper-studious fellow student by secretly stuffing cotton-wool in the earpieces of his stethoscope.

It was not only the consultants that provided the entertainment. Some of the patients, with characteristic Belfast humour, would play up to the gallery assembled around their bed. One of our medical consultants, with a host of sarcastic one-liners, won a joust with such a patient whom he felt was dominating the round with his witticisms. The consultant, as part of his examination of the patient, looked in his ear with an otoscope; the patient grinned at the group around his bed and asked, "Can you see my brain, Doctor?" To which our physician replied, without missing a beat: "My good man, this is an otoscope, not a microscope." One - nil, to the consultant.

Other than the bedside instruction there was no other formal teaching for junior doctors. You tended to learn from those just above you in seniority and experience. It was the, 'You can observe a lot just by watching,' school of learning, that quickly developed into the, 'You can learn even more by doing,' school.

As a houseman you were on call for your ward all the time, weekends included. You could get a few hours off here and there; the SHO or registrar would cover you on an afternoon to go and get a haircut. In the evening, if your ward was quiet, a fellow houseman might cover you for a few hours. However, overall, you took some pride in organising and looking after 'my ward.' Most of us regarded it as a year out of our lives when we could do nothing else; once you accepted that, it was straightforward. We did get two weeks holiday in each of the first and second six months of our tenure – this was our only official time-off.

After five o'clock, when all the other medical staff went home, you were elevated to the only show in town. You could get help from the registrar on call, but they were often so busy that you were basically all things to all people in your ward.

On the medical wards you were on take-in every fourth day for twenty-four hours. Take-in meant that all medical emergency admissions from casualty came to you. For surgical wards and surgical emergencies, it was every fifth day. All three junior doctors on the ward were involved during take-in. It was usually a full twenty-four hours non-stop work, with most of the next day spent mopping up. There were times of great physical and mental fatigue. I found when I was tired that I could still do technical or surgical tasks well – the first thing to go was sympathetic chat. For emergencies, one could always rise to the occasion.

I got into the habit of going to my ward at about eleven p.m. to 'put the ward to bed.' I would go over any patients the night nurse was worried about and anticipate any medication orders. The night nurses were all students; a first year on the women's ward, a second year on the men's side, with a third year as the senior in charge. These three looked after all fifty patients, with me as their back-up; talk about the blind leading the blind.

It was possible to prescribe Guinness (the popular, almost ubiquitous, dark beer in Ireland) as an evening tonic for patients well enough to partake. The Guinness company made a special one-third pint bottle for this purpose – 'Hospital Guinness,' as it was known. "There's eating and drinking in a glass of Guinness," as one patient said to me. To a degree he was right, it did contain a number of nutrients such as iron and vitamins. Many regarded it as a food and imbibed accordingly – much better than barbiturates.

A number of the older men were accustomed to sleeping with their flat cloth cap, 'duncher,' in place to keep their head warm. As you looked down the ward at night it was common to see one or two men fast asleep on their back with duncher in situ.

At night if you were called to see a patient, the night nurse might have a cup of tea and lemon toast ready. After you had dealt with the emergency, you had tea and toast as you went over the case together. Lemon toast was lightly buttered, sprinkled with sugar and squeezed lemon; it was very restorative. I think they sometimes did this to make sure you were *compos mentis*. Tea and toast at night was illegal, and if Night Sister found out there was hell to pay. The nurses had a system of phone calls that alerted them when Night Sister was out of her office and going around the wards.

We did not receive any formal or even informal evaluation during our houseman's year. You could pretty much tell by the demeanour and attitude of the consultants and sister if you were performing well. Toward the end of the twelve months, you got a short letter from the Dean or the Brigadier, I can't remember which, that said you had satisfactorily completed your houseman's year. You sent this to the General Medical Council, the licensing body for physicians in the United Kingdom, and thus became a fully licensed medical practitioner. As such, you could enter general practice or undertake specialist training.

In my six years as a junior doctor in the NHS I never received any evaluation or recognition, nor did I expect it – that's the way it was. There was one exception; after six months as an SHO in general surgery on Wards 19 and 20 at the Royal, the consultant wrote me a note (which I still have) saying: "Thanks for all your help. Good luck with your future career. You have no grounds for worry."

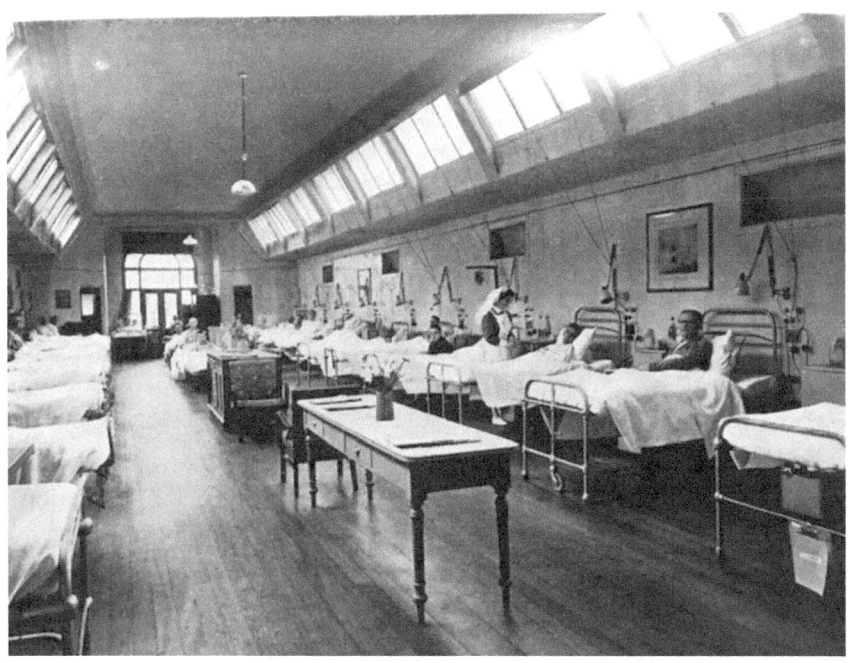

Ward 6, Royal Victoria Hospital, 1953
In the late 1950s curtain rails were installed around each bed

Chapter 10
Sudden Death Becomes Cardiac Arrest

In Belfast in the early 1960s when a patient's heart stopped in hospital the doctor was called to confirm death and fill out the death certificate. Occasionally attempts were made to restart the heart with the injection of a stimulant drug directly into the cardiac muscle using a syringe and long needle; inevitably without success.

The elements of modern cardio-pulmonary resuscitation (CPR) were finalised in the early 1960s. Initially these consisted of the ABCs: Airway, the correct positioning of the patient's jaw to keep the airway open; Breathing, mouth-to-mouth or tube-to-airway was superior to the old-fashioned Holger Nielsen chest and arm manipulations, and Circulation, chest compressions provided the best blood flow from the compressed heart. The final component, added later, was the D of Defibrillation. It was found that cardiac arrest after a coronary thrombosis or myocardial infarction (heart attack) did not mean the heart stopped beating – although it did in a small minority of cases. Rather, the heart muscle went into a chaotic, haphazard contraction pattern (ventricular fibrillation), which was ineffective at emptying the heart's chambers and circulating the blood. No pulse could be felt and hence 'cardiac arrest' was assumed to have occurred. Electrocardiogram (ECG), however, showed that ventricular fibrillation was the cause of 'cardiac arrest' in most cases after a heart attack. The only effective treatment of ventricular fibrillation was to restore the normal heart rhythm by giving an electric shock across the chest wall – defibrillation. The principle of CPR was to use the ABCs to sustain the patient until defibrillation was available.

Although the components of modern CPR trickled down to Belfast by 1963, there was no formal teaching in our medical school curriculum. It was Doctor Frank Pantridge, consultant cardiologist on Wards 5 and 6 at the Royal Victoria Hospital, who brought the first external defibrillator to the hospital in October,1963. At that time his houseman was John Geddes, who was the year ahead of me at Queens. The defibrillator was on a mobile trolley that could be moved to any ward and plugged into the electric outlet.

On the first of August, 1964, when my group began our houseman's year,

John Geddes became SHO (junior resident) to Doctor Pantridge, who decided there should be a system of mobile deployment of the defibrillator for the immediate management of cardiac arrests in the hospital. The job of organising this system and teaching the incoming junior medical staff the principles and techniques of CPR and defibrillation fell to John Geddes.

Sometime that August, John Geddes took each houseman (usually one to three at a time) for an introductory teaching session on the resuscitation cart and defibrillator in the side room of Ward 6. He informed us that patients who had previously been said to have suddenly died would now be deemed to have 'cardiac arrest' and, in selected cases, could be resuscitated, defibrillated and saved. He outlined and demonstrated the components of modern CPR and how to work the defibrillator. There were no educational objectives or mission statements or, indeed, any written material. Merely a clear and practical guide, lasting about thirty minutes, on how to do it. Thereafter, we just got on with it and became quite proficient. As we lived in the hospital all the time (our official title was descriptively apt, Resident Medical Officer) we were inevitably the first responders for all cases of cardiac arrest.

Cardio-pulmonary resuscitation is, in essence, an act of controlled violence, with three possible outcomes:

Failure – the most common result.

Pyrrhic victory – short-lived success, but the resuscitated person is only sustained with advanced life-support and intensive care; most of these patients die, hours or days later.

Triumph – in the grand scheme of things these are the individuals that make it worthwhile. One of the pioneers of defibrillation noted that patients who died after a heart attack were often found to have little damage to the heart at the time of autopsy. The cause of death was the ventricular fibrillation. He coined the term, *'hearts too good to die,'* to highlight this fact. This, then, was the *raison d'être* of CPR - the ability to save a life and restore the person to full health. Pretty brilliant stuff, if you could pull it off, and sometimes we did.

Doctor Pantridge, whose eccentric Ulster wit I have noted in other chapters, and who was known at 'Frankie P', was anxious to promote the benefits of CPR in the hospital. The following episode gave him the opportunity. One evening, Patrick Taylor, who was houseman to Doctor

Pantridge, wanted to have a few hours off to go to a movie with his girlfriend. He asked me to cover him and I agreed.

"Any problems on your wards," I asked.

"No," he said, "Just the usual, mostly recovering coronaries (heart attacks). All is quiet."

I should have known better. An hour later I got a call from the night nurse.

"Come quick, Tom, cardiac arrest, Ward 6."

I was in a nearby ward and was there within seconds.

"Mr. Currie, infarct two days ago," she said. She already had the board under the mattress and the other nurse had the resuscitation trolley and defibrillator at the bedside.

"OK, Doris, you do the chest compressions and I'll intubate him," I said. She was already on it, the nurses in 5 and 6 were steeped in CPR practice.

"Just stop for a second, while I pass the tube (the breathing tube into his air-pipe)," I said….. "OK, got it."

It was usually pretty easy to intubate someone who was, for all intents and purposes, dead. We quickly hooked up the ECG leads, which confirmed that he had ventricular fibrillation (VF). I tore open his pyjama top and applied the gel and defibrillator paddles to his chest.

"Everybody away" …. Shock …. Still VF …. Shock again …. Yes, back to normal heart rhythm …. Brilliant …. Well done, us.

It had only been about five minutes since Mr. Currie had arrested; the ideal circumstance to achieve successful CPR. I removed the tube from his throat, as he struggled to breathe on his own. He was back before he knew he was gone. The medical SHO arrived and I handed over to him, as I had other patients to see on my own ward. But, boy, did it feel good.

Later I went back to Ward 6 and was delighted to find Mr. Currie resting quietly and none the worse for wear. Nurse Doris and I quietly congratulated each other over tea and lemon toast. For both of us it was our first successful CPR – we were pretty chuffed.

Taylor returned and thanked me for covering him – his first trip outside the hospital in a month.

"Any problems?" he asked.

"Not really," I replied casually. "Just routine CPR and a life saved with sheer feckin' brilliance by one of the all-time great doctors with the name of T.F. Baskett."

"Up yours," he said. Taylor already had a successful CPR to his credit.

Taylor later recounted to me the events of the next morning's ward round. Dr. Pantridge was pleased that we had notched up another successful CPR and defibrillation. Addressing the assembled throng of juniors around Mr. Currie's bed, he emphasised the feasibility of rescue from cardiac arrest, saying, "If Baskett can do it anybody can do it".

I decided to take this as a back-handed compliment, which – coming from Frankie P – it was.

Individual cases can have a lasting impact, and one such served to confirm for me the value of this new approach to sudden death. A patient in his fifties, who I knew as the father of non-medical friends, was admitted with a myocardial infarction. The following day he arrested when we were close by, and therefore able to provide successful resuscitation. He went home and lived for many happy and productive years thereafter; this was the only case in which I had a personal link to provide long-term follow up.

Towards the end of the year I was houseman to the Professor of Medicine, Dr.Graham Bull, on Wards 3 and 4. During the morning ward round a sixty-year-old woman, who had been admitted the night before with a myocardial infarction, arrested in the bed next to us. The nurse and I went into our familiar and by now well-practiced routine; applied CPR and soon had her intubated and defibrillated. Professor Bull observed the whole scene with some bewilderment and, after we had the patient stabilised, he took me aside.

"Well done, Baskett," he said. "That was impressive, but should I ever have a heart attack and cardiac arrest in your presence you must promise me that under no circumstances will you subject me to resuscitation."

He was deadly serious. The patient was discharged home two weeks later.

I can only remember being involved in the three successful cases noted above. Our success rate in the general wards was about thirty percent, so I was probably at seven or eight unsuccessful cases. Certainly, I remember more failures than triumphs. It was notable that we succeeded in cases in which the arrest happened when staff were present and there was no delay in applying defibrillation.

In 1966, Pantridge and Geddes published the first eighteen months experience in the medical journal *Lancet,* showing that we had a thirty-one percent success rate across the hospital wards. At that time most hospitals were reporting success rates of less than ten percent. So, in retrospect we hadn't done a bad job, considering that our only training was a thirty-minute ad hoc tutorial.

Chapter 11
You Could Have Fooled Me

At about ten p.m. in early March 1965, I was standing in my room in the huts, naked and soaking wet after a hot bath.
The phone rang.

"Come quick, Tom, Ward 6, Mister Parling, cardiac arrest."

I pulled on my trousers and stepped into slip-on shoes. I was too wet to get into a shirt, so I just put on my white coat and ran.

Down the corridor of the huts …. turn left and sprint along the fence at the baseline of the tennis courts …. sharp right through the double-doors into the corridor under the wards, past the cafeteria on the left …. up the stairs, two at a time, and out onto the main corridor beside the entrance to Ward 6 …. through the heavy plastic double-doors into the ward. Half-way down on the left the curtains were pulled around Mr. Parling's bed.

In my defence I should recount the events leading up to this moment. I had just started on Wards 5 and 6 that morning and the night nurse had begun her block of night duty that same evening. Thus, both of us were new to the two wards of almost fifty patients. I had a habit of keeping a small notebook with the essentials of each patient. In both my notes and those of the nurse Walter Parling was a '*? myocardial infarction*' (suspected heart attack), admitted two days earlier. We were waiting for the results of his blood enzyme levels to confirm the infarction. As such, Mr. Parling had the potential for cardiac arrest due to ventricular fibrillation and was therefore a prime candidate for cardio-pulmonary resuscitation (CPR) and defibrillation – in which I was now well versed. Thus, the nurse's call that Walter Parling had arrested was not a big surprise.

I went through the break in the curtains and saw Walter Parling giving a good impression of sudden death, while the nurse was pushing the cardiac board beneath the mattress at the level of his chest. This was to provide some rigidity and facilitate chest compressions without the bouncing effect from the underlying bedsprings.

Fired with enthusiasm and life-saving endeavour, I gave him a solid pre-cordial (chest area over the heart) blow with my fist. He bounced a little and made what I took to be a terminal groan. I leapt up on the bed and with my knees beside his chest I started strong chest compressions. I should mention that at this stage in my life I was reasonably strong from my rugby-playing days.

Thump 'arrgh' .... Thump 'arrgh' .... Thump 'arrgh'

It soon began to dawn on me that Walter Parling was not behaving in the usual manner of those with a serious form of death. The resistance of his chest wall to compression, the consistent noises of distress and flailing arm movements suggested that he was, in fact, alive.

At this exact point the curtain was pulled back and the consultant, Doctor Frank Pantridge, appeared. A bachelor, he had a habit of dropping in to his ward in the evening on his way home after a nightcap at a local establishment. The scene that met his eyes was me, shirtless and sockless in a wet white coat, crouched in mid-CPR mode over an obviously live and increasingly resentful patient.

"Ah, Baskett, there appears to be a cerebral problem here – on both sides" he said, turned on his heel and left.

Further mitigation in my defence is necessary at this point in the story. It turns out that the medical and nursing staff had realised that Walter Parling was probably a fraud and making up his symptoms to gain hospital admission – a classic case of Munchausen's syndrome (see later). This was not transmitted to either the night nurse or me; to us he was a '*? myocardial infarction.*'

Nonetheless, it was pretty clueless of me not to seek his pulse before accepting a diagnosis of cardiac arrest and pounding his chest.

The nurse and I quickly moved to damage control.

"Well now Mister Parling you had a nasty turn there but luckily the nurse and I have got you back on an even keel. And Doctor Pantridge is clearly happy with how things have turned out."

We removed the cardiac board, dispatched the unused defibrillator, puffed up his pillows and tidied his bed.

"I've got a sharp pain in the left side of my chest," he whimpered.

"That's to be expected …. Nothing to worry about …. Now, get some sleep and don't have another turn or we'll have to repeat the treatment."

The next morning the ward round had the full complement of sister, junior doctors and students, with Doctor Pantridge at the helm. We came to Mr. Parling's bed, who regarded one and all, and especially me, with a suspicious and baleful stare.

"Ah, yes, the man who likes CPR, isn't that right Baskett?" Doctor

Pantridge turned to the patient. "How are you this morning Mister Parling? You look fit and well"

"I'm not, I have a very sharp pain in my left side when I breathe in."

"Right, in that case breathe in sparingly. Sister will arrange to have your chest X-rayed."

After the ward round we had the usual morning tea in the clinical room off the ward. Mr. Parling's enzyme results had returned as normal (no infarct), but his chest X-ray showed two broken ribs on the left side. Sister came in and told us that he had just left the ward, having signed himself out against medical advice.

"Well done, Baskett," Doctor Pantridge said. "An unorthodox approach, but you did manage to free up a bed, so that's something."

"No problem, sir, all part of the service."

"Don't push your luck, Baskett."

"Sorry sir, luck-pushing discontinued, sir."

I thought I saw him give a hint of a smile.

*

Munchausen's syndrome is a rare psychological disorder, more common in men, in which the patient seeks medical treatment for a factitious disorder. They become very skilled at mimicking the signs and symptoms of various medical conditions. They usually have multiple hospital admissions and often undergo several surgical procedures. The cause is unknown and there is no effective treatment.

Walter Parling was an Englishman in his fifties. His abdomen had multiple surgical scars, one of the telltale signs of Munchausen's, but unknown to me before I subjected him to my attack on his chest.

A few years later I read an article in the *British Medical Journal* that I'm sure documented his case. The author had collected the many dozen admissions to multiple hospitals in England over several years by a man of his age. The article described him as a potential record-holder for the number of hospital admissions – a Munchausen superstar. Although it did not include his Belfast admission, I'm convinced it was Walter Parling; he fitted the bill in every way. I think he had run out of hospitals to trick in England and had come over to Northern Ireland to try his luck. I probably sent him packing back to England; at least with some real pathology in the form of two broken ribs! Serve him right for making me look like a complete idiot.

Not my finest hour in the clinical arena, but I like to think I saved the Northern Ireland hospital system a lot of unnecessary expense.

(Some thirty years later, I met Dr. Pantridge at a medical meeting in London, where he was receiving an honour. We chatted after the meeting and, as I was about to leave, he said, "Look after yourself, Baskett, good men are hard to find." That's about as good as it got with Frankie P, and I was proud to be on the receiving end. He must have forgotten or forgiven my former ineptitude.)

Chapter 12
Wetting the Bed

Brendan Maguire was an orphan, and the same age as I was, when I admitted him to the medical ward during my year as a houseman. He originally came from the northwest of the Republic of Ireland, with the distinctive accent of that area, accompanied by a whimsical turn of phrase. He was of short stocky build, with thick black hair that grew in several directions at once. In general, he was a beguiling and likeable character.

His admission, for 'kidney function' studies, was arranged by the registrar (senior resident) from the medical outpatient clinic. Such investigations would involve a twenty-four hour collection of urine for analysis, blood tests and radiological studies. Nowadays, these would all be done as outpatient procedures. I think the registrar arranged for Brendan's admission to the ward because his history was so unusual and confusing. His only real complaint was that he had to get up at night two or three times to pee, and that he occasionally wet the bed – most unusual for a young man. Otherwise, his history and physical examination were normal. The registrar was worried that there might be some rare serious underlying kidney disease.

I had just finished writing up his chart, and was across the ward with another patient, when Brendan Maguire pushed his luck. I think even he would have known it was a long shot, when he tried to light up a cigarette as he lay in his bed. Sister came down the ward in a flash, with the wrath of God written all over her. Before she could speak, however, he greeted her with a disarming smile.

"Ah, Sister, here I am trying to light a cigarette with a match, when it would be much easier to do so with the light shining from your sparkling eyes – the eyes of a merciful healer, if ever I saw one."

I was stunned by his audacity and the flagrant degree to which he was laying it on – what a chancer! No Ulsterman would ever talk like that, and I was sure that sister would roast him. Instead, she got all flustered and, puffing up his pillows, mumbled, "There now, Mr. Maguire, don't be so forward – you should know you cannot smoke in hospital. We're here to make you better, so, and smoking won't help you, at all, at all."

"Ah, Sister dear, I am mortified to have unwittingly broken the rules. May the Lord above forgive me for upsetting such a wonderful person as yourself. Oh my, oh my."

"Just you rest easy now, Mr. Maguire, and remember there is absolutely no smoking on the ward."

So, to my surprise, despite chancing his arm to the hilt, he got away with it. After sister left his bedside, Brendan called me over.

"Jaysus, Doc, is there anywhere I can get a smoke? I'm dying for a drag."

In fact, there was such a place, but it would have to wait until sister was off duty. At the far end of each ward there were double glass doors that led onto a balcony overlooking the tennis courts and lawn that lay between the back of the Royal Victoria and the front of the Royal Maternity hospitals. These balconies were a throwback to the early days of treatment for patients with tuberculosis of the lungs – their beds were wheeled out so the patients could get fresh air. Although the Royal had never been a specialist chest diseases hospital, the same principle was occasionally applied to convalescent patients. Rarely, if a patient was well enough, they would be allowed out on the balcony for a smoke if sister was off duty. This did not happen often and, at a time when most men smoked, I don't remember nicotine withdrawal being a big problem with patients on the ward.

Luckily sister had a half day, so as soon as she left, I took Brendan out on the balcony for his smoke. It was a beautiful sunny day in late May.

"Jaysus, Doc, I really feckin' needed that," he said after his first few deep inhalations. He was one of those serious addicts, who inhaled the smoke deeply, and held it so long that very little smoke came out when he exhaled.

"Holy thundering jaysus, that's better – by, God, I needs me smokes," he said, after he had achieved nicotine equanimity.

Perhaps it was because I got him his smoke, or the two of us leaning companionably over the balcony railing – but after a bit of general chat, he opened up. Without the need for eye-contact between us, he looked out over the lawn and poured out his story.

"I didn't have a good time at school, Doc," he began.

I won't try and replicate his words here, as it would not do him justice, but the essence of his story was as follows:

He did not know the details of his early life in the Republic of Ireland. He had not been told about his mother or father – only that he was 'unwanted'. He was probably born to an unmarried young woman in one of the mother-and-baby homes run by one of the orders of Catholic nuns. The shame imposed on pregnant unmarried women in Ireland in the 1940s, when Brendan was born, was immense and crushing. The Irish government paid the church and the nuns to deal with the problem. Most of the babies born in these homes were adopted, but some were not – Brendan was not. He ended up at a Catholic residential school in the west of Ireland. Many of these schools provided a reasonable, if very disciplined, education.

However, as the world was to discover later in the twentieth century, there was in some of these homes and schools, rampant abuse of children in their care by both priests and nuns. Unfortunately for him, Brendan was in one such school. The children slept in a dormitory and as a nine-year-old, Brendan wet the bed. The response was to make him stand in front of the whole school at morning assembly, holding his thin rolled-up bed mattress over his head. It's hard to imagine what celestial guidance they invoked to justify this treatment of a little boy, but it happened repeatedly, as their response to his periodic bed-wetting mishaps during the ensuing years. He and the other boys were also subjected to harsh physical punishment. Eventually, at the age of sixteen, Brendan was able to leave the school and get a menial job at a brewery. He had bounced around from job to job since then, before ending up in the North of Ireland.

At the end of his story, I was pretty overwhelmed.

"It's not your fault, Brendan, none of it is your fault."

When I recounted Brendan's history to the consultant (staffman) on the ward, he went straight to see him. He pulled the curtains around the bed, while he and Brendan had a long talk. The senior man was scowling when he emerged from behind the curtain.

"This poor fellow doesn't belong here, he needs a different kind of help, and not from those bastards in the church," he said.

He was able to get a favour from his classmate, who was head of psychiatry at the Belfast City Hospital. (The Royal did not have a psychiatry unit). Brendan's transfer was arranged promptly.

Our tough sister, who now knew the full story, had tears in her eyes as she supervised Brendan's transfer.

"God love you, Brendan," she said. "I wish we could do more, but you'll get all the help you need at the City. We wish you well. You deserve the best."

"Ah, Sister, you're too kind, far too kind. Bless your heart. For you I might even try and stop smoking," he said with his winning smile.

"Away on with you now, Brendan."

I think Brendan was one of those people who coped with his powerless position and the aggression of others with humour. In order to survive he became an exaggerated stage Irishman – cracking the one-liners and over-the-top Irish banter. Behind that facade he was still a frightened little boy; one of many thousand victims destroyed by the church.

Chapter 13

"Peace Comes Dropping Slow"

As a houseman you were on your ward every day for most of the day. In addition, patients stayed longer in hospital and therefore had some days of early convalescence on the ward in contrast to the modern obsession with early discharge. As a result, you had time to get to know some patients quite well. Here are two that I remember:

Mr. Fergus O'Rourke was a widower in his early seventies from the South of Ireland. His daughter had married a man from Northern Ireland, and he was visiting her when he developed an acute flare-up of his chronic bowel inflammation. The end result was that he had an operation to remove a portion of his large bowel. I had admitted him to the ward and organised his early treatment. I was not involved in his surgery, but saw him every day of his ten-day postoperative care. He was a tall, courtly man with thick white hair and an attractive soft-spoken southern Irish brogue. He had been a school teacher and there was a gentle dignity about him.

The hospital doctors did not have name labels then and we were often just referred to as, the doctor, or the houseman. One day he asked me, "May I have the honour of knowing your name?" It was such a quaint request and put so nicely that I felt foolish for not having introduced myself by name before. Over his last few days in hospital, I would occasionally sit on the side of his bed and chat when we had a chance. He talked of his years as a teacher.

"Are you familiar with the poetry of William Butler Yeats?" he asked.

"Yes," I said, "We did some of his poems at school. Of course, I remember his *Lake Isle of Innisfree.*"

"Indeed, so," he said. "His best-known, and though it was one of his earliest it remains one of my favourites. You just can't beat the rhythm and sound of it. I think he's the finest poet in the English language – at least of this century."

"Well," I replied. "The Irish have always had a knack of mastering and improving the English language."

"That's kind of you to say," he said.

That evening I looked up some of Yeats' poems in my copy of *A Pageant of English Verse*. The next day I was able to trot out the opening lines of

When You are Old; "When you are old and grey and full of sleep, and nodding by the fire, take down this book, and slowly read …."

"Ah, yes," he said, obviously pleased at my remembrance, and finished the entire poem without missing a beat. His voice and recitation were of the best Shakespearean acting standard.

On Friday afternoon, while he was sitting in the chair beside his bed Mr. O'Rourke had cardiac arrest. The registrar was on the ward and started the resuscitation. By the time I joined them from the woman's ward next door, Mr. O'Rourke was on his back on the floor with the registrar and nurse doing cardio-pulmonary resuscitation. I quickly hooked up the electrocardiogram and defibrillator, but the ECG did not show the hoped-for ventricular fibrillation (which we could treat), it just showed no heart action at all. We shocked him but could not get any response. We gave up after five shocks. The nurses brought extra screens around, but you can only hide so much from adjacent patients in a twenty-bed ward. It was such a sad and undignified end for a man I had become fond of. I was taken aback that night when I suddenly shed some tears for Fergus O'Rourke, just before I fell asleep.

The autopsy showed that he died from a pulmonary embolus – a known complication after surgery, when a blood clot forms in the veins of the leg, breaks loose, and travels up to the lungs. When it is large, as it was in Mr. O'Rourke, there is no treatment, and CPR and defibrillation are not effective.

It seemed such an unjust death for this lovely old man; CPR on the floor and an autopsy. I was glad his wife wasn't alive to know how his life had ended. He should have died in his sleep after an evening spent with Yeats' poetry. Perhaps, *Lake Isle of Innisfree*, one of his favourites:

"And I shall have some peace there, for peace comes dropping slow."

*

I first met Mr. Michael McNaught when I was houseman on a surgical ward. He was a short stout man in his mid-fifties, who worked as a clerk in the office of a big coal company in Belfast. He had recovered from a recent operation to remove part of his colon (large bowel) for cancer. Unfortunately, there was spread of the cancer outside the bowel, so he was being admitted for chemotherapy, which I was to organise and give.

"Hello, Mister McNaught, how are you?" I asked.

"I'm rightly, Doctor, I'm here for my dose of Harpic."

Obviously, his sense of humour was intact; Harpic was a well-known toilet bowl cleaner. A typical light-hearted Ulster approach to a serious situation.

"You know what this is all about, do you? Has the treatment been explained to you?" I asked.

"Well, yes, I think so. I had a growth in my bowel removed last month. They said there was a little spread which should be cleared away by the Harpic medicine."

"That's about it. I have to give you the medicine into your veins, so I will set up an intravenous drip, and the drug runs in that way. You will get one dose each day for three days. The drug is called Five Fluorouracil, or 5-FU for short."

"I prefer the short name," he said, "As in FU too, ha ha – not aimed at you, of course, Doctor."

I went over the possible side effects of nausea and hair loss. He only had a sparse periphery of grey-brown hair, but even the loss of this would be significant in the days when men did not shave their whole head, as some do now.

As we talked during his three days in the ward, I came to know he was a bachelor and that, outside his work, his main interest was racing greyhounds. His latest 'grue,' as greyhounds were known in Belfast, was called Basil, and he was training for his first race. There were two racing venues in Belfast: Celtic Park, which was close to the hospital, and Dunmore Stadium on the other side of town. You often saw men exercising greyhounds on a leash around the streets of Belfast – 'walking the grue', as it was known.

The regimen for 5-FU called for three courses of the drug at four-week intervals, so I gave Mr. McNaught all his treatments during my three months on the ward. He tolerated the drug pretty well, but did lose most of his hair. Overall, he remained his usual cheerful ebullient self, and I enjoyed working with him on each of his three-day stays. For his last session he arrived in particularly good form.

"Basil got a third in his first race at Dunmore Stadium last week," he said proudly.

"Good for Basil, well done to both of you," I said. "I too have run at Dunmore."

"You're having me on."

"No, I came second in the half-mile at the Ulster Youth Athletic Championships, which was held at Dunmore Stadium in my last year at school."

"No kidding," he said. "I bet Basil would have youse all beat."

"No contest," I agreed.

Some eighteen months later I was doing six months as an SHO (junior resident) in general surgery, when I encountered Mr. McNaught again. It was a sad reunion and I didn't recognise him at first. We were on take-in when he was admitted in the late afternoon from the follow-up clinic – he was on his last legs. The stout man I had known was replaced by a severely wasted, jaundiced body. His cheeks and eye sockets were sunken. He was in pain. He recognised me first.

"I'm glad to see you, Doctor. Do you remember me? You gave me my Harpic medicine."

"Of course, I remember you Mister McNaught – how's Basil?" Mentioning Basil was the surest way of letting him know that I did remember him.

"Basil is rightly," he said. "I had to get a friend to take him over, but he's had a couple of wins this year."

"I'm sorry you're having such a bad time," I said.

"It's no one's fault. But I'm just about done for, Doctor."

"Can you drink fluids and keep them down?" I asked.

"I'm OK with some fluids, but no solid food. I'm thirsty all the time."

"Where is your pain?"

"All over. But worse in my stomach and back."

From his chart I saw that he had secondary spread of his cancer just about all over his body, but mostly in his liver and spine.

"I'm going to get you comfortable first." I put up an intravenous drip, at least we could help his thirst by getting him hydrated. I added some morphine to the IV to help his pain.

The nurse who came on in the evening was Angela Mooney, a third-year student nurse who was in charge for the night. As luck would have it, she had been on the ward with me when Mr. McNaught was having his chemotherapy. She remembered him as the likeable, cheerful, optimistic character he was back then. Now he was a shell of a man in terminal pain. At least he was with a nurse and doctor that he knew, and it seemed to comfort him. Angela and I talked in the kitchen office area that separated the two wards.

"God love him, he's on the way out. We've got to control his pain. Whatever it takes," I said.

"I'm with you all the way on that," she said. She was close to tears, and I wasn't far behind. We were both affected by the sad transformation of Michael McNaught.

"Let's hit him with the Brompton cocktail," I said.

"Right," she replied, already using her key to open the drug cupboard that contained the narcotics.

The Brompton cocktail originated at the Brompton Chest Hospital in London as palliative pain control for patients with terminal cancer. There were various mixtures – ours was the full-strength version, with heroin, cocaine, alcohol, chloroform water and syrup. It was taken by mouth, so that the pain of intra-muscular injection was avoided, and Mr. McNaught didn't have much muscle left.

"I'm going to prescribe it 'ad lib', so get as much of it into him as you can." Ad lib meant the nurse could give the drug freely at her discretion.

"Anything you need medically, you get me," I said. I wanted him to have only familiar faces with him at the end.

"OK, thanks," she said.

We put him in the bed just inside the entrance to the ward. At night it was close to this bed where the night nurse sat, when she had a chance to sit, with a small lamp beside her. This was always a reassuring sight for the sicker patients at that end of the ward.

After Nurse Mooney had got some of the cocktail into him, I visited again.

"How are things now, Mister McNaught?"

"Much better, Doctor, thanks," he was half asleep.

"That cocktail's pretty good stuff, isn't it? Even better than Guinness," I said.

"Dead on," he said, "I'm OK now."

"I promise we'll keep you comfortable. Nurse Mooney here is one of the best."

"She is that," he murmured.

Angela Mooney called me at about four am. "He's gone," she said. I came up to the ward, confirmed his death and filled out the death certificate. Afterwards we had a cup of tea together in the kitchen.

"He was such a decent wee man,' she said, "To see him like that, it doesn't seem right."

"It never is, but you made him comfortable, Angela, so he had a gentle departure. And he knew us both, so that helped him too. I think we did OK by him. Life can be a bugger sometimes."

"It certainly can," she sniffed.

"Let's have another cup of tea."

*

In medicine you remember the failures and sad cases more than the successes; especially if you get to know the patient as a person, rather than as just a medical diagnosis and treatment. One of the most dramatic, a failed CPR resuscitation, you could pass off as a technical failure if you didn't know the patient or their relatives. If you got to know the patient, as I did with Mr. O'Rourke, it was quite different and could be upsetting.

There is a modern tendency to advise professional counselling after bad outcomes in hospital and elsewhere. I don't think this is necessary or a good thing in most cases. The best counselling comes from going over things with those who share the same work environment. This is preferably done over a cup of tea on the ward, in your room with a friend, or a pint or two in the pub with a colleague. That's how we dealt with it – after that, you just got on with it. It seemed to work. Gallows humour could be part of it.

HL Mencken, the quotable American journalist of the early 20th century, said: "The only praise worth a damn comes from those who work at the same bench." I think this applies to an understanding of bad outcomes at work – it needs to be someone from the same trade, as it were. It's one of the reasons doctors and nurses are often helped by marriage to someone in the health field – I certainly was. I believe this applies to all areas of endeavour in which bad outcomes can be life-threatening, such as Firefighters, Paramedics and Police.

That said, sad memories sometimes still intrude into a dark corner of the night.

Chapter 14
"*Though Wise Men at Their End Know Dark is Right*"

It was a quiet time on the ward, just after lunch and before the afternoon visiting hour.

"Plop" – Mr. Gordon McFee made his statement in dramatic fashion by throwing a turd over the curtain surrounding his bed. It landed on the floor in the middle of the ward beside the nurse who was hurrying to bring the now too-late bedpan to his bedside. I was with a patient across the ward putting up an intravenous drip, and looked over just in time to see a second faecal missile arc over the curtain rail. The poor first year student nurse was mortified as she scrambled to clean up, anticipating severe chastisement from sister. In fact, sister was quite understanding, "Timing is everything nurse," was all she said while helping to clean up Mr. McFee and his bed.

Two days before this encounter I had admitted Mr. McFee to the ward after he had a stroke at his home. He was eighty years old, tall and thin – almost gaunt. His hair was white and unusually thick, as were his bristly eyebrows. From a neighbour we learned that he was a widower, lived alone and had two children who worked and lived in England.

The cause of his stroke was probably a bleed into one side of his brain which caused paralysis of the muscles on the opposite side of his body – hemiplegia is the medical term. In this case his left arm and leg were paralysed. At his admission examination I could not get a history as he had also lost his power of speech; he kept trying but could only produce the sounds: 'Mmmm…Mmmm…Mmmm…'

"Mr. McFee, you are in the Royal Victoria Hospital. You have had a stroke and that's why the muscles on your left side are weak and why you cannot speak. I think you can hear me OK. There's a good chance your muscle strength and speech will improve – but it will take time. In the mean time we will get things stable for you. Then we will organise treatment at a special unit to help you recover."

This was pretty much the standard routine for the initial management of stroke patients in the 1960s. In a few days a consultant in physical medicine would come and see him and arrange for further treatment in the rehabilitation unit at the nearby Belfast City Hospital; as always, the problem was availability of beds in that unit.

Shortly after the turd-hurling incident I went back to examine Mr. McFee and see if there were any changes in his clinical condition to explain this outburst. His blood pressure was not abnormally high and a repeat neurological examination was unchanged. But he was very upset and clutched my white coat with his functioning right hand. He was remarkably strong and I had difficulty prising his fingers loose. He grabbed my coat again and fixed me with a gaze so intense that it was unsettling, coupled with his urgent and repeated refrain: "Mmmm…Mmmm…Mmmm…" He was trying desperately to get something through to me, and I thought I knew what it was – he was raging against his condition and did not want to live like this. I could see his point. I acknowledge that this was my interpretation of Mr. McFee's feelings from behind the barrier imposed by his stroke. Even though I was an inexperienced and indestructible twenty-three-year-old, his plight and what I concluded from his compelling stare and incoherent pleading noises had a profound effect on me – I can still see him quite clearly.

One week later, with his medical condition unchanged, he was transferred to the stroke rehabilitation unit. For the remainder of his time on our ward he seemed passive and resigned – uninterested in anything. I do not know his long- term outcome, but I suspect he just gave up.

*

The title of this chapter comes from the Dylan Thomas poem, *"Do Not Go Gentle Into That Good Night,"* which urges defiance of death. Another line advises the elderly to, "Rage, rage against the dying of the light." This theme and one or both of these lines is repeated in each of the six verses. The single line that speaks for the acceptance of death is the one I chose for the title of this chapter: "Though wise men at their end know dark is right." I admit it was only my personal interpretation that Mr. McFee was not raging, "…against the dying of the light," but rather hoping the lights would be turned off completely – that, "…dark is right."

Having reached Mr. McFee's age group one naturally wonders about the end of life. It seems that for the elderly the following outcomes await: one quarter will die from an incurable cancer, one quarter from a cardiovascular accident (heart attack or stroke), and one half of us will eventually succumb to "progressive dwindling." A degree of dwindling is normal and acceptable; it is the progressive far end of the dwindling spectrum that most of us fear – which includes loss of controlling motor functions and the dementias.

When I was a junior doctor one of the main medical ethical debates concerned therapeutic abortion, which at that time was a criminal offence and only permitted in very rare circumstances. After much discussion in the 1950s and 1960s it eventually became widely available in civilised societies. The major impetus for its acceptance was the carnage of illegal backstreet abortion. I think the current debate on medical assistance in dying (MAID) is at the same stage the therapeutic abortion controversy was fifty years ago. To a degree this is a product of the success of modern medicine, resulting in a larger proportion of the population living to old age. The end result is more old people reaching the far end of the dwindling spectrum, unable to live independently and being housed in so-called care homes – some of which are substandard. It seems difficult now for those working in hospitals and care homes to provide the old-fashioned gentle exit by allowing people to stop eating and drinking, and provide comfort care along with liberal doses of the derivatives of opium; although this has been the way of things for centuries, even millennia. After all, the job of medicine is to prolong life, not to prolong death.

Medical assistance in dying is now legal in Canada; unfortunately, it is not available to the largest cohort of people who need it. To be granted MAID you have to be *compos mentis* and able to give fully informed consent. The main group that would benefit from MAID are those who have descended into late dementia or advanced neurological degenerative disease, including stroke – none of whom can give informed consent. This is even more compelling when one realises that about half of those who live beyond eighty-five will develop dementia. When I ask people if they were to reach the stage when they could not carry out some or all of the basic functions: feed themselves, bladder and bowel control, recognise and communicate with family, read or write – I have not met anyone who would not emphatically choose a dignified exit with MAID, rather than be housed in a semi-vegetative state. This can only be achieved by allowing people to prepare an Advanced Directive, listing the circumstances under which they would request MAID; it could and should be as common as making a will. At present advanced directives are useful to define conditions for which one does not want active treatment, but they are not valid for MAID. Why should politicians, sometimes not the brightest or most exemplary citizens, be allowed to dictate personal medical decisions?

I write this in my early 80s, still in reasonably functional if imperfect nick on most fronts. However, to use a football (soccer) analogy, I am in extra time and facing a penalty shootout that can only have one result – and that's fine by me. But I should be allowed to give advance directions and define the conditions for a dignified exit if necessary or, as it were, to choose the circumstances under which the deciding goal is scored.

****

One might think that we would approach the end of the houseman's year with relief – the end of 80-100-hour work weeks and continuous call. In fact, it was tinged with a degree of nostalgia and sadness. Although we were not all firm friends, groups of us had become very close. We had been together for seven years; some of us had started together in grammar school at the age of eleven. We had faced and overcome the same academic and social hurdles, with varying degrees of success. On paper, at least, we were now fully qualified doctors, and after the last year we had some reasonable practical credentials as well.

There was to be one last collective effort – the Houseman's Concert. This was an annual event put on by the housemen, with a mixture of ribald songs and sketches – most of which took off and lampooned the senior medical and nursing staff. I had a moderate talent for mimicry, so I played a number of roles and was one of the script writers. It was our final group hurrah, performed in the hall of the Bostock House nurse's residence in July, 1965. It ran for three nights to standing room only audiences and was a huge success. As I look over the programme and scripts now, it was a bit paediatric and certainly politically incorrect, but at the time we thought it was great, and some of it was. We charged admission and from the proceeds we had one last group dinner and drinkathon.

Once you made the decision to start medical school the next seven years were mapped out for you, provided you cleared the intermittent examination hurdles placed in your way. Now, after all these years together, it would end – we were about to be forced into the adult world. Friendships forged in good times and in bad times are the strongest. It would never be the same again.

Chapter 15

General Practice 101

When we finished our houseman's year, we became fully licensed general practitioners. No further training was required but most of those committed to a career in general practice would do further hospital house jobs, six months obstetrics and six months paediatrics – both areas not covered in our houseman's year. For those of us taking specialty training we could, during our holidays or time off, do locum general practice work. There was plenty of it about and we needed the money.

In Belfast the Contactors Bureau was set up to coordinate this activity, namely, to provide locums for those GPs who wanted their night or weekend calls covered – house calls were a big part of general practice in the 1960s. Patients rarely went directly to Casualty (Emergency), but usually called their doctor first. The other frequent request was to cover GP surgeries (regular office or clinic sessions) in which, ironically, surgery was not involved. Longer locums of one to two weeks duration were arranged individually as the GPs got to know us.

When we had a night or weekend off from hospital work, we could take house calls. These were directed through the Contactors Bureau and we carried a rather crude radiophone, augmented with calls made from public phone boxes. The most common surgeries (office hours) we covered were those in the evening after our hospital day had finished. Most GPs had an evening surgery to accommodate those who worked – time off work to go and see the doctor was not routinely granted by employers. We received £1 to cover a one-hour surgery, and half of that, ten shillings, for a house call.

An understanding of the people's lexicon in Ulster general practice was important. Much of this we knew from our hospital work, but some was applicable mainly to frontline practice. Some examples and their implications follow:

"He's got the green gollies." Applied to small children with green infective snot coming from the nose. Implications were an underlying sinusitis or chest infection, possibly needing antibiotics.

Two of the more theatrical ones involved vomiting: "She was up all night calling for Hughie," or "She was up all night calling for Ruth."

These were, in a way, brilliantly onomatopoeic and as such gave a clue to the type of vomiting – as in:

Huuuheee – the more prolonged projectile-type vomiting.

Ruuuth – the shorter dry-heave type.

Another emetic variation was the commonly used "boke" – with the productive "wet boke" and the minimal or low-volume "dry boke."

Pain had its own local lexicon. "Stoon" was a sharp shooting pain, often referred to as "a terrible stoon" or "a wicked stoonin' pain." The word "chronic," pronounced in parts of Belfast as "cranik," as applied to pain could be confusing. For example: "The pain was very bad all evening, but in the night it became something chronic." One might think this meant that the pain was at its worst in the evening and became less, though persistent, in the night. In fact, the opposite was true, "chronic" was used to describe an acute worsening of the pain.

To "thole" meant to tolerate something unpleasant, usually pain: "I was able to thole the pain for a while, but then it got so bad it was chronic, so it was."

"Beeling" described sepsis or suppuration, usually in a wound, boil, or abscess. "The cut on my finger is beeling, so it is."

One became wary of the patient who learned a few anatomical words and used them to show that he was knowledgeable about medical matters and therefore not to be trifled with.

"I've got this pain in the left side of my chest – I think it could be my cardiac heart or possibly my gastric stomach. The wife said it might be my renal kidneys, but I think that's a long shot – what do you think, Doctor? I'm just glad there's no sign of the yellow jaundice."

It would have been tempting to reply with one of the Ulster forms of rhyming slang to indicate stupidity: "Your arse in parsley" or "Your bum's a plum." Or the one used to describe someone who was being really ridiculous: "Your bum's out the window." Of course, one would never use such language with a patient, but I thought they should be included here as some of the more colourful items in the Ulster lexicon.

There was considerable variation in the standard of facilities available for general practice in Belfast. The best had a receptionist, a nice waiting area, organised patient records and proper examination and minor treatment rooms. The worst, the one's we were most often asked to cover, had a waiting room, a doctor's office and no receptionist. These practices were in the impoverished areas around the Royal. The waiting rooms were sparse, with no magazines which would have been stolen. As a majority of patients smoked, ashtrays were provided, also at risk of theft. In one practice I covered there were cocoa tin lids nailed to the table in lieu of ashtrays. In some rooms the examination couch was covered in boxes of old files and dust, and obviously unused for its original purpose. The office hours were listed, for example, seven p.m. to eight p.m., and an unlimited number of patients would turn up. There were no appointments and a receptionist, if one existed, was never at the evening surgery.

From a patient's point of view, it was survival of the fittest. A typical doctor–patient encounter was as follows:

Patient enters the doctor's office.

"Hello, what's your name?"

"James Milligan, Doctor." Doctor starts to write the name on a prescription.

"What can I do for you Mister Milligan?"

"I've got a bad case of the bronchites, Doctor."

"Are you coughing up any yellow or green spit?"

"Yes, Doctor, something fierce, so I am."

In order for one to keep up, all of the above dialogue should have occurred before the patient's bottom hit the seat in front of you. At the mention of green spit, you filled out the rest of the prescription for an antibiotic.

"I'll just have a quick listen to your chest." This was done if one was gilding the diagnostic lily, and to make a pretence of doctoring. The patient pulls up his shirt .... A quick listen to the bases of the lungs .... Deep breath in .... If any crackling noises, the chest infection is confirmed.

"Yes, Mister Milligan, you do have a chest infection."

"The bronchites then, Doctor."

"Yes, the bronchites, Mister Milligan."

"Thought so."

"Here's a prescription for a strong antibiotic. How many days do you think you need off work?"

"Usually takes a full week, Doctor."

"Here's a note for four days."

"Fair enough, Doctor."

"Send in the next patient." Total time – four minutes at most.

This would be followed by the sound of scuffling in the waiting area, until the next successful challenger burst into the room.

"Hello there, what's your name?" And so on.

It didn't always go as smoothly as this. Some patients became quite indignant if you suggested examining them – even with a cursory stethoscope to the chest. "My doctor's not an examining doctor, he's a prescribing doctor." One could usually anticipate this response by the depth of dust and the number of items stored on the examining couch.

Others, even if amenable to examination, made it difficult. Among older people there was a habit in winter of wrapping layers of thick red flannel around their chest and abdomen. This was to provide warmth and to protect the lungs and kidneys from "winter inflammation." Unwrapping this to examine a chest or abdomen was both time-consuming and a nasal challenge – the same flannel was often used for several weeks.

Pernicious anaemia is rare, about one in five hundred people have it. The treatment in the 1960s was by injection of the deficient vitamin B12. The drug's name was Cytamen, and it came in a small, one millilitre glass ampoule with an attractive rose-coloured liquid. For some reason a lot of patients in Belfast were on it, certainly more than one in five hundred. It seemed to be prescribed as a magical tonic and many patients were addicted to their monthly injection. It was common for them to bring the prescribed ampoule of Cytamen to the surgery for you to inject. One of these almost defeated me. A man brought his ampoule for injection, which would be given into the muscle on the outer side of the thigh or into the upper, outer quadrant of the buttock.

"Right, just drop your trousers," I said, after loading the syringe.

"I'm not dropping my trousers, my doctor just gives it straight into my leg here," he said, indignantly, pointing to his outer thigh.

"Through your trousers?"

"Yes, through my trousers, it works fine," he said, as though I was a half-wit. He was obviously not going to budge. To my shame, after looking furtively over my shoulder, I gave him his injection through his trousers into the thigh. In my defence, I did wipe the target area of the trousers with an alcohol swab pre-injection. In his defence, it seemed to work fine.

Many patients took over-the-counter remedies, one of the most common being DeWitt's kidney pills. These were advertised for all and any ailment of the urinary system, and were purportedly particularly good for "sluggish kidneys." The key ingredient was methylene blue dye which turned the urine an impressive blue colour, confirming that the medication was getting to the root of the problem. One elderly woman, in whom I diagnosed a bladder infection and prescribed a suitable antibiotic, came back the next day complaining that my medicine was useless because it hadn't changed the colour of her urine.

People didn't talk about "mental health," they complained about "being bad with their nerves" or perhaps, feeling "low in spirits" – mostly anxiety and depression. In truth, many had a pretty hard existence and there was much about which to be anxious or depressed. In the 1950s the barbiturate drugs were popular as anti-anxiety or minor tranquillizer medications. By the early 1960s these were largely replaced by the benzodiazepine drugs, librium and valium, and these became the most widely prescribed drugs of all.

The name of the medication was not always written on the bottle of pills the patient received. Thus, renewing prescriptions could pose an identification problem: "You know the one, Doctor, the wee pink pill." Although the categories of drugs available were much less than to-day, there were a lot of drug manufacturers making different varieties of the same drug. In the 1960s, in the United Kingdom there were 105 such companies, so the numbers, colours and shapes of pills and capsules was considerable. Luckily there was a booklet with a colour identification chart of pills and capsules, and another booklet with a short synopsis of each drug, the *Monthly Index of Medical Specialties* or *MIMS*, sent to each doctor in the UK. One carried this at all times, or you were completely lost in the world of prescription renewal.

It really was medicine on the fly. One had to trust one's instincts and hope that the patient's symptoms and appearance would provide a clue to any potentially serious ailment. If so, you sent off one of the preprinted form letters, *Request for Outpatient Consultation*, to the appropriate specialty clinic at the hospital, where the patient would get a thorough examination. Apart from minor ailments or conditions that could be rapidly treated or prescribed for, this was how one dealt with the fifteen to twenty patients who could turn up for the one-hour clinic.

In fairness to the GPs whose practices we covered, they knew their own patients and probably had the clinical antennae to pick out potentially serious illness from the mass of apparently mundane complaints.

Chapter 16
The Dog Comes with the Practice

My first encounter with general practice in the country started immediately after my houseman's year. At nine in the morning, on Sunday the first of August, 1965, I handed over to my successor on Wards 3 and 4 and headed south to the town of Newry, County Down – 40 miles (65 kilometres) from Belfast. I was to be locum tenens for the month of August, live in the house of the general practitioner and use one of his cars. My stipend for the month was £135 ($380.00), which would pay for the honeymoon in Spain after our wedding in early September. Five days back in Belfast to organise myself before the nuptials should be more than adequate – what could possibly go wrong?

Over the next five years I would do two weeks GP locum per year in Newry, Newcastle and in a small village outside Belfast. In addition, I did some shorter locums and a lot of weekend call and GP clinics in and around Belfast, as outlined in chapter fifteen.

I bought a GP's black bag with various pull-out compartments for drugs and essential equipment. At the first practice they loaded me up with the necessary medications and bits and pieces. I still have the bag which, in essence, contained a small pharmacy of pills and injectables (including morphine and other narcotics) along with the syringes and needles necessary for emergencies. In addition, there was a collection of instruments, sutures, bandages, strapping and slings to deal with minor injuries.

The drugs for injection were in glass ampoules, which came with a small piece of metal that had a serrated edge – a miniature saw. This was used to 'saw' the junction of the thin top with the main body of the ampoule, allowing you to snap off the top with your finger and thumb. Modern ampoules are made with an easily snapped-off top, so the saw is no longer needed.

The final vital item was a Swan Vesta matchbox filled with threepenny coins ('thrupenny bits'). This was the price of a phone call in a public phone box – often needed as many homes did not have a phone.

The morphine came in ampoules labelled as: 15mg (1/4 grain). This was acknowledgement of the relatively recent change, in the early 1960s, by the

British Pharmacopoeia from the Apothecary to the Metric system of measure. In the 1960s it was still common for 15mg of morphine to be referred to as 'a quarter of morphine', in recognition of the former equivalent one quarter grain dosage. (Advice from a senior GP to me: "When you go out to your first emergency call, give the patient a quarter of morph and take a quarter yourself.")

Not only was morphine available but also its stronger relative, diamorphine (heroin), in certain circumstances. I covered a practice in which a terminally ill, elderly woman, Mrs. Jane McNulty, with a large cancerous growth in her neck was being looked after at home. She and her family of five children were determined that she would see out her last days at home, rather than in hospital. Pain control had become difficult and, when I got involved, she was on heroin injections three times a day. The district nurse gave the morning and afternoon injections and I administered the late evening dose. Compared to morphine, heroin was thought to provide better pain relief with less nausea and sedation. It also gave a feeling of well-being and serenity. Obviously, the potential for addiction in a terminal illness was not a consideration. (Ironically, heroin was not available in the United States, at least not to the medical profession – except illegally and commonly on the street).

After a few days of this routine, I arrived one evening to find all her children assembled in the living room. Could they meet with me before I went upstairs to see their mother? They knew that conventional medicine had no more to offer, other than the palliation we were giving. A little sheepishly they told me they had consulted a hermit who lived deep in the woods and who had a reputation as a healer. He provided, for a ten-shilling fee, special plasters impregnated with herbs and other secret ingredients that could apparently heal serious skin diseases refractory to 'ordinary' medicines. They had described Mrs. McNulty's condition to him and were told that only when the tumour broke through the skin of her neck would his plasters be effective and draw out the tumorous growth and associated poison. As the skin over the tumour was now beginning to erode, should they consider using these plasters? What did I think?

I was taken aback as I was not aware of the healing hermit. These were decent people, trying to do the best for their mum. I could tell they really didn't believe in the hermit's plasters, but maybe there was something in it, and they didn't want to leave any stone unturned. Of course, they had heard stories of the hermit's miracle cures of chronic sufferers. It was an understandable, 'Hail Mary', last ditch effort, to be considered in their desperation and helplessness as they kept their death watch.

Earlier in my career, (I had now been a doctor for all of four years), I might have been quicker to condemn the hermit and his plasters as mere quackery. Instead, I said I understood why they had consulted the hermit and that many would do the same in their position. We talked about plasters and the chance of them curing their mum and the possibility of damaging the skin and worsening her pain. They described their own experience with mustard plasters; in their generation they were still occasionally used for aches and pains and chest colds. When applied, the mustard produced local heat and could give a feeling of relief; it could also cause blistering of the skin. In the end they decided not to use the hermit's plasters. I think they just needed to talk it out with someone who purportedly knew about these things. They did most of the talking. I was beginning to learn that it is often better to turn on the 'receive' button, rather than to go into full 'transmit' mode – sometimes referred to as 'listening medicine.'

Palliative Care was not well developed in the 1960s – the pioneer work of Cicily Saunders was just becoming known. Most of us were not very good at it. Mrs. McNulty was still alive when I left the practice and returned to work as a junior hospital doctor.

General practice in the country was different from that in the city. In the doctor's surgery (clinic) you could do more; such as suturing lacerations and removing simple 'lumps and bumps'. In addition to the usual clinic hours there were a lot of house calls, as most patients did not have a car. Directions to homes could be difficult when you were a stranger to the area, for example:

"About half a mile past the grey barn on the left side of the town road and then right at the big oak tree. Be careful, half-way up the lane to the house there's a big boulder that's part of the path, which could take out the oil pan on your car if you don't go slow." At night I always told them to keep all the lights on in the house so I could spot it – no GPS or cell phones and, often, no house phone.

In some of the country homes the house call consultation could be quite formal. You were greeted at the door and thanked for coming. The reason for the call was presented and you were escorted to the bedroom of the patient. If it was a child, the mother stayed with you, otherwise you were left alone with the patient. When you returned back to the living area there was a basin with warm water, a small towel and a fresh bar of soap, so the doctor could wash his hands. (The adults of the pre-antibiotic era were very particular about cleanliness and often had an exemplary approach to the prevention of infection.) A cup of tea was offered, and you gave your opinion and advice. It was all very civilised. For other calls, access to the house was across a very functional and manure-strewn farm courtyard. The local GP kept a pair of Wellington boots in the car for these farms, and had left boots for me – luckily, they fitted me.

In one country locum the dog came with the practice. I was to live in the doctor's house and look after his dog – a yellow labrador retriever called Rory. As I was a doggie person and labs were my favourite breed, this was a plus. When I arrived, the doctor was poised and itching to get away in a large modern car and take his family on holiday. He had left me his second car, which was ancient and had a broken starter motor.

"Can you use a handle to crank and start a car?" he asked.

"Yes."

"Show me – you know about the thumb, do you?"

My two older brothers had old cars, so I was used to starting the engine with a handle. In particular, the thumb must not wrap around the handle in a natural grip but be placed on the same side as the fingers – to prevent a potential thumb fracture if the handle kicked back, as it often did. I demonstrated my technique to his satisfaction.

"One other thing, Rory will not allow anyone in the car unless he has been driven around in the car with me." So, the GP, Rory, and me (at the wheel) drove about half a mile together before the doctor left on holiday. Rory and I became instant best friends and he accompanied me on all house calls. Sitting up in the passenger seat he really did have quite a noble profile. His presence was very useful, as I often left the car running for short stops to avoid having to hand-crank the engine. Rory's attendance ensured the integrity of the car and its contents.

On one occasion this had dramatic results. Each week the local GP went to the Pharmacist's shop on the main street, parked outside illegally and went in to sign repeat prescriptions. I was to do the same and was told that the police knew the car and would overlook this weekly parking transgression. Accordingly, I left the car running for the few minutes I was in the shop. When I came out there was a small crowd of locals and tourists around my car, at the centre of which was a young and very pissed-off looking policeman. He presented me with a parking violation ticket. Rory was in the driver's seat, looking out the open window with a triumphant gaze. Apparently, the constable had reached in to turn off the ignition key, awakening a snoozing Rory in the passenger seat. He leapt at the constable's arm, but luckily didn't break the skin; it was more a loss of face that annoyed the young policeman. He was unmoved by my explanation. I went to the police station and recounted the event to the sergeant. He apologised for not telling the new constable about the parking anomaly and tore up the ticket. "But," he said, "the doctor is too cheap, he should have fixed that starter motor months ago." I couldn't disagree.

The phone in the hall rang at about three a.m. – why is it always three am? I stumbled down the stairs from the bedroom, there was no phone extension upstairs.

"Is that the doctor?"

"Yes."

"Could you please come to see my husband – he's having one of his asthma attacks, and it's a bad one."

"Yes, of course, where are you?"

"We're here on holiday in the caravan park. My name is Jane Watson."

"I'm on my way, Mrs. Watson. Put all the lights on in your caravan, so I can find you."

The caravan (trailer) park was popular for summer holidaymakers in Newcastle – situated, as it was, 'Where the Mountains of Mourne sweep down to the sea.' It was also close to the famous Royal County Down golf course.

I quickly dressed and picked up my bag. Rory had a pee on the neighbour's hedge before leaping into the passenger seat with his usual enthusiasm.

I found the caravan easily, as a beacon of light in an otherwise dark slumbering settlement. Poor Jeremy Watson was in classic acute asthma mode; sitting up on a chair with his shoulders hunched forward over a table in the dining area of the caravan. He had the frightened look of a man fighting for his life – which in a way, he was. In acute asthma the airway passages in the lungs narrow suddenly (bronchospasm) in response to a trigger – in this case probably summer pollen. Mr. Watson was in his forties and, I was later to find out, a school teacher. He was making short inspiratory gasps followed by a long wheezing expiratory effort. With bronchospasm it is getting the inhaled air back out through the narrowed air passages that it most impeded. The effort of the prolonged expiratory wheeze is exhausting and, along with inadequate oxygenation, causes great distress in the sufferer. No matter how hard they work they still feel, and are, short of breath. I remembered these patients from casualty and always felt sorry for them.

"Hello, Mister Watson, no need to talk. I'm sorry for your troubles. I'll get you relief in a few minutes." He nodded. I quickly listened to his lungs with my stethoscope and confirmed the classic high-pitched expiratory sounds of acute asthma.

From my bag I got a ten millilitre (ml) syringe and opened an ampoule of aminophylline with ten mls of the drug, which I would give into Jeremy Watson's vein.

"I'm going to need you to keep one arm still for five minutes while I inject this drug into your vein. The medicine will relax your airways and give you relief. So, get into your best position for that." He was already holding the edge of the table with his hands, which made it easy to place the rubber tourniquet around his arm and find a good vein. Into the vein with the needle, release the tourniquet and inject the aminophylline at two mls a minute over the next five minutes.

Aminophylline was a drug that should relax the bronchospasm and give near instant relief of his breathing distress. It had to be given slowly or it could drop his blood pressure to a critical low; hence the slow injection over five minutes. This can be a long time when you're trying to keep the needle in the vein of a desperate gasping man; but he was resolute in keeping his arm steady.

It worked – by the time I removed the needle from his vein his bronchospasm was lessening.

"Thanks," he said, "Bless you. It must have been the pollen."

In the 1960s the chronic control of asthma was not as good as it is now with modern inhalers. Asthmatics were at the mercy of an allergic response to one of many potential triggers, precipitating an acute attack of bronchospasm. It was common to see these patients in general practice or casualty.

As I drove back to the house with Rory, I felt pretty pleased with myself; this was real doctoring. How gratifying it was to be able to relieve someone's acute distress, as if by magic.

"What do you think of that, Rory?"

"Well done, Baskett," he would have said, if he could.

Chapter 17
In the Name of the Father

Bernadette Murphy was already an experienced participant in the world of reproduction when she was admitted to the Royal Maternity Hospital (RMH) in the spring of 1967. As the thirty-four-year-old mother of seven, plus two miscarriages, she knew the maternity routine only too well. On this occasion, however, her pregnancy was not routine; her labour was premature, very premature. She was only twenty-six weeks, compared to a full term forty-week pregnancy. In 1967 there was no neonatal intensive care in Belfast, so a baby that premature would not survive. Not only was the baby too early, it was coming bottom (breech) first – a more complicated delivery. The senior resident that night was busy with a caesarean section, so the care of Mrs. Murphy fell to me and all of my, so far, two months experience in obstetrics.

Mrs. Murphy was a short dark-haired woman who looked older than her years. She was cracking on in labour but well in control.

"Mrs. Murphy, you know your labour is very early."

"I know, Doctor."

"The baby will be very small and may not be fully mature."

"I know, Doctor, it's too soon."

I wanted to be realistic but not brutally so. There was also the slim possibility that she might be a month further on and the baby have a borderline chance of survival. She progressed rapidly and coped without pain relief, aided by the young midwife's support. The baby was so small and her labour so efficient that the delivery required no skill, merely the gentle receipt of a tiny bundle. It was a boy weighing about two pounds and obviously not viable.

I quickly cut the cord and placed him on Mrs. Murphy's abdomen, where the midwife had a warm towel waiting. There was a heartbeat of about sixty and he made occasional gasping efforts, but was clearly not going to survive beyond a few minutes. We wrapped the towel around him as Mrs. Murphy cradled him to her chest.

"God love your wee soul," she said through her tears, as the midwife and I watched, each of us through moist eyes.

With the labour ward so busy, and the midwife and I both non-

Catholics, we had forgotten to alert the hospital priest about the potential need for baptism. I knew how important it was for Catholics that baptism be performed after birth if the baby might not survive. Apart from her name and the size of her family I knew Mrs. Murphy was a Catholic – in those days the patient's religion was marked prominently in their chart. It was clear that her baby was going to expire very soon; he barely had a heartbeat and his gasps were only occasional now.

"I'm very sorry, Mrs. Murphy, but he's just too early and too small."

"I know he is, Doctor. God has chosen to take him early."

"I'm not a Catholic, but would you like me to baptise him – I know it's allowed."

"Yes, please do, Doctor."

"What would you like me to name him?"

"What's your first name, Doctor?"

"Tom or Thomas in full."

"Please baptise him Thomas – it's a good name."

The midwife brought over a metal bowl with clean water. As Mrs. Murphy cradled him in her arms, I dropped water from my fingers onto his head: "I baptise thee Thomas, in the name of the Father, and of the Son, and of the Holy Ghost."

Not a dry eye in the house, as young Thomas stopped gasping and his heart stopped beating.

"Thank you, Doctor and nurse – that was lovely."

"Bless your heart Mrs. Murphy."

Although the hospital priests were very efficient and always available, it was important in obstetrics to be aware of so-called 'heretic' baptism; that performed by a non-Catholic with the use of any water, not just holy water. Such was the importance of neonatal baptism that the legitimacy of the heretic variety had been endorsed by the Catholic Council of Trent more than 400 years before. At the heart of the Catholic Church doctrine was the concept of 'original sin' by Adam and Eve, and that every newborn infant was imbued with this sin which could only be removed by baptism. If not, according to St Augustine, the infant's immortal soul was condemned to eternal damnation; this was later softened to the soul of the infant going into a form of limbo from which it might be saved by God's mercy. I have always felt this to be one of the church's more illogical and harsh rulings.

That said, it was very important to devout Catholics, and on the occasions that I performed neonatal baptism I found it to be a very moving experience. I considered it an honour to be able to provide some solace for the parents at a desperately sad time. Another feature of the strong religious belief held by many of our patients was the concept of 'God's will.' Mrs. Murphy's quiet acceptance that God had chosen to take her newborn son to heaven early was a commonly expressed and comforting sentiment among women who had a stillbirth or neonatal death in that era.

On one other occasion I carried out baptism using my own name for the baby. With no forewarning the baby was born with multiple lethal abnormalities and was to die, mercifully, within minutes. The parents were Catholic and asked if I would baptise their baby with my own name. So, I performed heretic baptism for another doomed Thomas.

In the days before ultrasound and prenatal diagnosis parents and health personnel knew almost nothing about the baby before birth. The first question many mothers asked at delivery was "Is the baby okay?" often before asking whether it was a boy or a girl. Nowadays most parents in developed countries know more details about their baby before birth than the paediatrician.

The only other time a baby was named after me was the first delivery I ever did. I was a medical student doing my obstetric rotation in the summer of 1963. For my first delivery I was assigned a patient in labour under the care of a midwife. I had to stay with the patient for her entire labour and carry out, under the tutelage of the midwife, all the functions of a midwifery attendant. My patient was a nineteen-year-old having her first baby. After thirteen hours, two midwife shifts and two short food/bathroom breaks for me, she finally came to delivery. At that time, we had no epidurals for pain relief, only narcotic injections and nitrous oxide gas inhalation. My poor patient had unrelenting back pain with her contractions and for the last four hours of her labour I was instructed to rub her lower back with cream during the pains. I don't know if it did any good, but my hand was numb at the end of it all. She was delivered of a healthy boy, ostensibly by me, but with the senior midwife's hands on top of mine to guide the appropriate manoeuvres.

When the midwife enquired what the young mother was going to call her baby the patient asked me my first name. Up to that time I had been formally referred to as Mister Baskett the medical student. The patient, who was only three years younger than me, said she would like to call her son Thomas. I was quite chuffed but thought it must be quite a common occurrence; we had after all just shared a very close and intense thirteen hours.

As far as I know it never happened again. So, other than my two short-lived neonatal namesakes, there is only one other Thomas named for me; he would now be well into his fifties and, I hope, still going strong.

Chapter 18

Never Again, Doctor

I first met the redoubtable Mary McAteer half-way through her first labour, which was for her a miserable experience. I had spent the day on the wards and clinics of the Royal Maternity Hospital and came on duty for the labour ward at six p.m. There were six labour rooms and, as usual, I went round each one to get up to date on the evening's potential problems.

"Good evening, Mrs. McAteer, how are you getting on?"

"Feckin' deadly, Doctor, now that you ask. This is not how they said it would be in the antenatal class. These pains are desperate, so they are, and not getting me anywhere."

"I'm sorry you're having a bad time. Let me check you and see how things are going."

"These pains are a real bugger, Doctor, mostly in my back and Jean the midwife here tells me I'm going slow 'cos it's my first labour, and it will be my only labour, I can tell you …. Ahhhh …. Jesus Christ …. Mother of God …. Ahhhh …." She was consumed by another pain and clearly having a very tough time of it.

I examined her and found her cervix (neck of the womb) to be five centimetres dilated – halfway to the full dilatation of ten centimetres. In keeping with her severe pains and backache the baby's head was descending with the back of its head (occiput) towards the back of the pelvis – the dreaded occiput-posterior position. This occurred in about one-in-six first labours, which was usually more intensely painful and prolonged.

The options for pain relief during labour in the 1960s were threefold. Encouragement and breathing exercises could be helpful in the short term, but hard to sustain and ineffective over many hours. Narcotic injection coupled with a sedative also had its limitations in a long labour. Patient-controlled breathing of nitrous oxide (laughing gas) was helpful for short term relief towards the end. We did not have epidural anaesthesia (injection of local anaesthetic around the nerves at the base of the spinal cord), which was to revolutionise pain control during labour from the 1970s on. Thus, our ability to provide Mrs. McAteer with decent relief for her long and painful ordeal was limited.

I did, however, have one ace up my sleeve, for which she was the ideal patient. We had recently started a trial with different local anaesthetics using a new-to-us technique called paracervical block (PCB). It was simple and was carried out during a normal internal (vaginal) examination. It involved using a long thin guide through which local anaesthetic was injected into the tissues at the sides of the cervix to block (freeze) the nerves that transmitted the pain of the contractions. For the woman it was virtually painless to receive, apart from the disruption of an internal examination.

The result could be spectacular, with almost complete relief of pain within a few minutes. The problem was it only lasted one to two hours, but it did give them a chance to sleep and regroup. When it wore off the pains returned as bad as ever. I gave her small doses of intravenous narcotic intermittently to try and tide her over, but with limited success. I was also able to give her another PCB – two was the limit. Nevertheless, poor Mrs. McAteer, who resumed her unrestrained and extensive vocabulary after the block had worn off, had about another ten hours before her delivery at four a.m. She was exhausted and demoralised when we used forceps to deliver her of a baby girl. Her daughter, to be called Erin, was almost nine pounds in weight and healthy from the word go.

First-time mothers stayed in hospital for at least seven days after delivery. At twenty-six years, Mary McAteer was older than most first-timers from her part of Belfast. She was what was known in Ulster as 'a big frame of a woman.' This was not a derogatory term and did not denote obesity, but a tall, well-built, solid physique. I saw her each day and warmed to her uninhibited, forthright, no-nonsense approach to motherhood and life in general. She was delighted with her daughter but made no bones about how awful she had found her labour and delivery.

"I know you and the midwife did your best, but apart from those short breaks when you injected me, and bless you for that, it was just feckin' misery. And my arse is still aching from the cut you made to help her out with those metal forceps things. I don't think I'll ever be the same, so I won't. But my wee girl is a treasure, so she is. None of us know what our mother's go through to have us."

I could only make sympathetic noises, which seemed pretty hollow under the circumstances.

"No harm or offence to you, Doctor, but this is the last time you'll see me here. I won't be back. Never again, Doctor."

It seemed to me that the large families many women had in that era were due to a combination of selective amnesia, heroism, and a lack of contraception. Mary McAteer certainly had the heroism but seemed unlikely to develop the selective amnesia.

*

Two years later I was covering Doctor Gerry Murphy, a Belfast general practitioner, for weekend calls. On the Friday evening, about nine o'clock, I got a call to a house off the Falls Road where a two-year-old girl was sick with fever and a cough. Mrs. McAteer opened the door to both our surprise. I explained that I was covering her GP for the weekend. We were pleased to meet again and gave each other big hellos.

"Are you still at the Royal Maternity, Doctor?"

"Yes," I said, "I do some GP cover on my time off."

"Well, thank you for coming, you'll see a big change in the wee baby you delivered, but to-night she's sick and we're worried."

"Let's have a look."

She led me into the front room where, on the sofa, her husband sat with little Erin clinging to his big frame.

"Eamon, this is the doctor I told you about, the one who delivered Erin. He's covering Doctor Murphy."

"Thanks for coming, Doctor, wee Erin's feeling a bit poorly, so she is," he said.

Erin glanced over her shoulder at me and then quickly resumed the tight grip on her Dad, burying her face into his neck.

"She's had a cough all day," said Mrs. McAteer. "But this evening it got worse with green spit, and when I took her temperature, it was 103 – that's when we decided to call."

"Quite right too," I said. "I'll just have a listen to her lungs."

Without having to move her I placed my stethoscope and listened through her fever-dampened dress to the back of her lungs – which confirmed a few crackles and wheezes. She wouldn't allow much else, so I didn't push it; there was nothing to be gained by trying to examine a crying, struggling child. I had enough to go on with.

"I think she's got a bit of bronchitis, so I'm going to start her on penicillin. I have a sample here of Pen V syrup, which will tide you over until you fill this prescription to-morrow morning. And here's some Panadol (an aspirin-type drug) to keep her fever down. Try and get her to drink some fluids. I'll check in again to-morrow."

My reason for checking her the next day was, in part, my own insecurity with sick children. I was always worried about missing something serious, particularly meningitis. In addition, I thought Erin would be more amenable to a thorough examination the next day. In those days most GPs didn't send children off to the Casualty/Emergency department without good cause.

I called back again late the next morning. Her husband was at work and things had improved with Erin. Typical of small children, they seem at death's door one day, and up and about right as rain the next. I checked Erin over as she sat on her mother's knee.

"I think she's on the mend, but make sure you complete the course of penicillin."

Erin got down off her mother's knee and went to play with her toys in the corner of the front room.

"Doctor, I'm really glad to see you again. I haven't forgotten how good you were to me, even if it was a bit of a losing battle. I still can't forget how bad labour was for me. Would you like a cup of tea, Doctor? Have you time for a wee chat?"

"I would and I have," I said, sensing she wanted to talk. She brought in the tea and we sat for a bit, watching Erin play.

"Erin seems like a great wee girl," I said.

"She is, so. And my friends wonder why I'm not having another. Round here, once you start, it's almost an annual event. But I still have nightmares about the last time."

"I know, and I'm very sorry about that. No one can promise, but first labours are almost always the hardest. After that they are usually much shorter and easier. I know that's easy for me to say, but it's true."

"So, everyone tells me, but I'm still fearful. Eamon is a good man and a great father and husband, but I know he would like a son. He doesn't say so, but I know it, so I do. Perhaps someday, but I'm still not ready, so I'm not."

"Have you talked to your own doctor about this?"

"Doctor Murphy, yes, I have, and he's very understanding. At the moment he has me on the pill. It's to control my bad periods, so he says, and it means I don't have to worry about getting pregnant."

This was quite common in the Catholic population, who were forbidden effective methods of birth control. The Church allowed use of the pill for gynaecological conditions, but not for birth control. Many GPs made a pragmatic decision to prescribe the pill for women like Mrs. McAteer, ostensibly for reasons other than contraception.

Mrs. McAteer was just warming to the topic. "Then last month, just after Erin's second birthday, the priest came to visit. After the usual small talk, he asked if everything was all right with me and Eamon, and were we expecting another happy event in the family? That's the way the buggers' check up on you, nothing subtle about it. I got angry and told him happy events were our own family's business and nothing to do with his celibate church. Then I told him, saint's preserve me, that I was assuming they were celibate. He nearly choked on his tea, the cheeky young bugger, and him barely shaving – what does he know about family? You know, Doctor, there's birth control and there's church control and the two should have nothing to do with each other."

Well said, Mary McAteer. Good for you. Not many would stand up to a priest, but Mary McAteer was a formidable woman and not going to be bossed about by anyone.

Chapter 19
Just Getting a Few Things for the Children's Supper

The call came in to the receptionist just before the ten am. deadline. The general practitioner I was covering had a system for house calls, and patients knew to call in before ten a.m. After that the doctor was out and about doing the calls and was unavailable, until he returned to do his afternoon surgery (office/clinic) at one-thirty p.m.

The receptionist handed me the list of calls:

"You may want to take this one first, Doctor", she said. It was from a Mrs. Eileen McIntyre on a street off the lower Shankill Road within a mile or two of the Royal Maternity Hospital, where I was in my second year as a Senior House Officer (junior resident). Mrs. McIntyre had called to say she was eight months pregnant and she thought her 'waters had broke'.

I drove my small Hillman Imp car (similar to a Mini) to her street. It was typical of the mill houses built for workers during the industrial development of Belfast in the late nineteenth/ early twentieth century. A continuous row of terrace houses, two up two down, built directly onto the pavement. A tiny yard off the kitchen at the back was just big enough to accommodate an outside loo.

The door to number nineteen was ajar so I knocked, pushed it open and said, "It's the doctor here."

A small, six-year-old girl appeared with brown hair in two short pigtails and green snot coming from one nostril. The latter presumably the reason she was not at school.

"Is your mother here, she called the doctor?"

"Me mammy's not here, so she's not."

"Where is she then?"

"Down the street at the shop."

"What's your name?"

"Maisie."

"Well Maisie, you hold on here and I'll go down and get her."

I strode down the street with my black bag feeling a bit miffed at Mrs. McIntyre's absence from the home, having put in for an urgent call. It was a cool day in March, but the sky was clear and sunny, brightening the usually grey and dismal landscape. The street was a cul-de-sac, at the end of which two houses had been made into a small shop that sold groceries and other basic essentials. I pushed into the shop and was about to chastise the only customer present when I saw the meconium–stained* fluid running down the inside of her right leg. She was a classic wee Belfast woman of this area: about five feet tall, thin and wiry, dressed in a thick blouse, short tight skirt, with bare legs and flat shoes – known as 'flatties'. Her whole outfit had seen better days. She was the type of woman I frequently saw in the clinics at the RMH, and whom I had come to admire. They raised large families in very difficult circumstances, retaining, for the most part, a wicked Belfast wit. I always felt that they accepted their difficult lot because everyone they knew was in the same boat. They were one of the reasons I chose to do obstetrics.

"Mrs. McIntyre, I'm the doctor you called, Doctor Baskett, I'm covering while your own doctor is on holiday."

"O jeez, Doctor, I'm sorry not to be at home, but I'm just gettin' a few things for the children's supper. I know I might have to go to the hospital."

"That's OK Mrs. McIntyre." There were two problems here. First, she was a month early with ruptured membranes and likely to go into premature labour. Second, there was meconium staining of the fluid which could mean the baby was 'distressed', as in not getting enough oxygen, and perhaps the umbilical cord was being compressed. I took her bag of groceries and we walked back up the street. "Just take very small slow steps Mrs. McIntyre and keep your legs together. Are you having any pains?"

"Not much, Doctor, just the beginnings."

As we slowly made our way back to the house, I took a quick history.

"How many children do you have?"

"Five, this'll be my sixth, and one miss." (miscarriage).

"How old are you?"

"Thirty-two."

"Any other health problems?"

"Not really, Doctor, just a bit tired what with the children and all that."

"Where are you going to have this baby?"

"At the Royal."

---

*Meconium: fetal bowel movement that stains the normally clear amniotic fluid around the baby a green-brownish colour

It turned out she was booked to have her baby at the RMH, but I had not seen her at the clinic so far. She had her first and fifth babies at the RMH, and babies two to four at home. This was in keeping with the maternity policy in Belfast at that time. First and five and higher number pregnancies were at greater risk of abnormalities in labour and therefore booked for hospital delivery. Others, at lower risk, were looked after at home by the district midwives and GPs.

When we got back to the house another small person had appeared from the back room; 'wee Jimmy,' was two and a half, firmly sucking his thumb, big brown eyes, but no chat. His thin yellow-brown hair could not cover his prominent bat ears. (Local joke: 'As he grew up, we weren't sure if he would walk or fly.') He was in short trousers, hitched up in a way that made one trouser leg much longer than the other.

"I need to examine your tummy Mrs. McIntyre, if you could just lie down on your couch."

I examined her abdomen and no sooner had I laid on my hands than she had a contraction which was quite firm but, stoic that she was, she only winced. So, it looked like she was in early labour. When the uterus relaxed, I could feel that the baby was lying bottom first or breech. This increased the chance of the umbilical cord falling down below the breech – the dreaded cord prolapse. This is the quintessential obstetric emergency because the cord, via which oxygen is provided to the baby, can be compressed and limit or stop the oxygen supply.

"Mrs. McIntyre your baby is coming bottom-first and with that dark staining of your amniotic fluid the baby's umbilical cord may be under pressure. I'm sorry, but I need to examine you internally to make sure. It's important for your baby that we know right away."

"Whatever you need to do, Doctor."

I took a pair of sterile gloves from my bag and had no choice but to examine her in front of the two children – I used the rug on the couch to cover as much as possible. Maisie, who seemed to have inherited her mother's calm common sense, held wee Jimmy's hand and two sets of eyes fixed me with an unwavering suspicious stare.

My examination confirmed the worst: the cervix was already dilating, so she was in labour, and protruding through the cervix was a loop of cord. Luckily, it was pulsating strongly, so the cord was not being compressed and the baby was getting its usual oxygen supply from its mum. But this could, and indeed would, change very quickly. With her sixth baby the labour was likely to progress rapidly causing the breech to descend and cut off the baby's oxygen line. I had to get her to hospital quickly where she would need an immediate caesarean section to deliver the baby safely. I decided the quickest way was to drive her there myself, rather than call and wait for the ambulance. I would phone the RMH and have them prepare the operating theatre.

"Right Mrs. McIntyre, you are in labour and the cord is in front of the baby, but it's not being compressed so your baby is OK at the moment. But we need to get you to hospital at once, where your baby will have to be delivered by caesarean. I'm going to call the hospital to be ready for you and I'll take you in my car. Get Maisie to fetch your neighbour and don't move an inch."

"Maisie go next door and get Mrs. Black."

"Right, ma."

Not far up the street was a phone box – no one in these houses had a home phone.

I rushed out, taking the match box full of 'thrupenny bits' that I kept in my bag for these occasions; threepence being the cost of a local call in a public phone box. I phoned the RMH, got the switchboard and asked them to page urgently the senior tutor – the most senior of the junior staff. He was an Ulsterman but had been to a private school in England and had a slightly upper crust accent and a cynical view of the world.

"Mike, its Tom here.... "

"Ah, still fulfilling the general practice needs of the local citizenry for fun and profit I assume."

"No Mike, this is serious, listen: I have a thirty-two-year-old, with five children, at thirty-six weeks, breech, in early labour with ruptured membranes, meconium staining, cervix four centimetres with cord prolapsed, but pulsating nicely at about 130. I'm going to bring her in my car. I'll be there in five minutes or so. Have a trolley and midwife in the front lobby and the theatre ready for an immediate caesarean."

"You've got it, Tom." He hung up.

Cynical or not, when the chips were down Mike was solid as a rock.

When I returned to the house Mrs. Doreen Black, the neighbour, was in attendance and taking charge. She was short, sturdy, and confident. In her late forties, her children were all grown up or at school.

"Hello, Doctor. Don't you worry, I'll have Eileen's children all sorted and fed when her others are back from school. And supper on the table for her man, Gordie, when he gets back." In these areas of close-quartered housing neighbours could always be counted on to help out.

"Thanks, Mrs. Black, that's a great help."

"Happy to do it."

"Mrs. McIntyre, does your husband work at Mackies?" (A large foundry nearby and a big local employer)

"Yes, he does."

"I'll have the hospital phone him so he can come straight there."

I was able to check the baby's heart rate by leaning over her abdomen and applying my ear to the small five-inch-long cylindrical obstetric stethoscope. With Mrs. McIntyre's thin abdominal wall, it was easy to find the fetal heart, which happily was still solid in the 120-130 beats-per-minute range.

"Your baby is still fine, a good strong heartbeat."

"There you are, Eileen, your baby's a good un," said Mrs. Black encouragingly

"I need one more thing, Mrs. Black, a small towel that I can fold into a pad."

In addition to the threat of physical compression of the cord, the other potential problem arose if the cord prolapsed right out of the vagina. Even if it wasn't compressed, the colder temperature outside the body could cause spasm of the blood vessels in the cord, effectively cutting off oxygen transfer. I folded the towel into a pad and told Mrs. McIntyre to use both hands and hold it firmly to herself so that nothing could come out of her front passage. (In those days we used the terms 'front passage' and 'back passage', rather than the anatomical words for vagina and rectum.)

Now I had to get her into my small car. I went out and quickly cleared the back seat and moved the door and front seats to allow access. I returned and lifted Mrs. McIntyre, carried her out and somehow manoeuvred her into the back seat. Luckily, even pregnant, she only weighed about eight stone (110 lbs).

In the back seat I had to hitch her skirt up to her hips so she could hold the towel pad against herself to prevent the cord popping out. There she lay, flat on her back, clutching the pad, with her knees bent and her feet up against the side window – 'flatties' still in situ.

"Right, Mrs. McIntyre, we're off."

"Jeez, Doctor, here's another pain – they're getting stronger."

"Just hold on and breathe" -- brilliant advice, honed by years of training and movie watching.

"Hope the newspaper photographers aren't out in force today," she said, confirming that her Belfast wit was intact—a good sign. "I don't want to appear like this on the front page of the *Telegraph*."

"Never worry," I said. "It would be page three at the most."

"You're a sketch, Doctor, so you are."

"Keep holding that pad tight."

"I am, Doctor."

"We're almost there." Luckily the traffic was light, with no hold-up at the one traffic light en route. A stop at the traffic light might have encouraged closer scrutiny from pedestrians with many potential interpretations – none of which would have enhanced either of our reputations. Off the main hospital road there was a short circular driveway to the front of the RMH. As I drew up the doors opened, and Sister McNally and a pupil midwife burst through pushing a trolley. Thank goodness, Sister McNally was a seasoned campaigner who had seen it all.

"Right, Doctor, what have we got?"

"Mrs. McIntyre, breech, cord prolapse, moving on in labour," I said as I lifted her out of my car and onto the trolley.

Sister took her hand and said, "It's all right Mrs. McIntyre we're all here and organised. Everything's going to be fine."

"I need a pair of gloves, lubricant, and a big sheet."

"Got them here Doctor," said Sister.

"Jeez Doctor, I think somethings coming out," said Mrs. McIntyre.

I put on the lubricated glove and asked her to remove the pad. Right enough, the cord was pushing out. I cradled it in the palm of my hand as I replaced it high in the vagina and with my fingertips pushed up on the breech, trying to keep it from compressing the cord against the pelvic bones. Only someone who had borne five children and with great fortitude could tolerate such a medical assault without anaesthesia.

At first my heart sank when I couldn't feel any pulsations, but as the contraction faded, the uterus relaxed, and I was able to push the breech higher. The pulsations returned but only to about sixty to eighty. The cervix was now more than half dilated and it was going to be a losing battle if we couldn't get the baby out very soon.

To preserve a modicum of dignity for Mrs. McIntyre, Sister put the sheet over her and around my shoulder and arm. I walked, crouched over beside the trolley as they pushed it through the front hall to the lift (elevator), which had been commandeered and was being held open by the hospital porter. Up one floor and off the lift to the right were the double doors into the labour and delivery unit. First on the right in the unit was the caesarean section operating theatre. Inside was Mike and a midwife, both already scrubbed and gowned. The anaesthetist, Doctor Fintan McCarthy, was at the head of the operating table, drugs prepared and ready to give the general anaesthetic. Sister put a cap and mask on me and wrapped a gown round my body to provide a semblance of asepsis. Otherwise, the usual operating room protocol had to take second place to the circumstances.

Despite her remarkable fortitude Mrs. McIntyre began to tremble as her resolve faltered.

"Oh, God…. Oh, sweet Jesus …. Where's my Gordie?"

The poor soul, less than forty minutes ago she had been in the shop and here she was in an operating theatre with a doctor's hand up her front passage, facing a major operation.

"Mrs. McIntyre, your baby is still OK, I can feel his heartbeat. Everyone is here and ready to make sure he's safe. (Generic 'he'). We have to get you up across from the trolley onto the table, and I'm coming with you – you're stuck with me."

"God love you, Doctor."

To get her to the operating table I had to clamber up beside her on the trolley and shuffle across with her, keeping my hand in place, before I could take up my position crouched at the side of the operating table.

"Doctor McCarthy will just put a wee needle in your arm and give you the sleeping medicine. When you wake up, you'll have your baby. Everything will be OK, I promise."

Mike threw a sterile sheet over me as he prepared the abdomen. I kept my now very cramped hand in place, pushing against the breech to protect the cord as best I could.

"Still eighty to ninety between contractions," I said.

"Good to hear you're still alive under there," Mike replied.

The anaesthetist gave the anaesthetic drugs followed by intubation.

"All right Mike, you can cut now," he said.

"I can't feel any pulsations now." This is really bad – the baby needs to be out and breathing within four minutes to avoid potential oxygen deprivation and brain damage.

"I'm going to do a lower midline incision", Mike said. This was not as cosmetic as the transverse 'bikini' incision but was quicker to perform, and would save one or two minutes.

"I'll warn you when I'm cutting into the uterus with the scalpel, at which point you should remove your fingers if you don't want your surgical career to be cut short – literally".

Sharp inhalation of breath from me; as my fingertips were up inside the lower part of the uterus this was brutally realistic advice.

"OK, cutting in now."

I removed my hand and crawled out from under the sheet. Mike was just bringing the breech of the baby through the uterine incision along with the tangled cord. He quickly delivered the rest of the baby in textbook fashion. It was a boy and Mike passed him into the towel-covered arms of Sister McNally who took him to the resuscitation cot. She rubbed him vigorously and to my delight he began to cry loudly. Wee brother Jimmy was no longer bottom of the family pecking order.

There was palpable relief all round, most of all from me. Mike reverted to superior English mode:

"Right, Baskett, well done. Now kindly remove your septic personage from my sterile operating theatre. And do try and keep the level of medical mayhem in the local community down to a dull roar, there's a good chap. Still and all, a bit of a triumph – all part of the rich pageant of obstetric life."

Indeed, it was.

Chapter 20
A Criminal Offence

I was the SHO (junior resident) on duty for the gynaecology ward at the Royal Victoria Hospital one evening when I got a call from the houseman (intern) in Casualty (Emergency Room).

"You'd better see this one promptly, I think she has been in the hands of the backstreet brigade. She's nineteen years old, about nine weeks pregnant, with bleeding and cramping. Her temperature is 104 (40 degrees Celsius) and her lower abdomen is super tender. So, I think she has a septic abortion, she's pretty ill, and I don't like the look of her at all."

She clearly needed admission so, rather than examine her in the often-chaotic Casualty department, I arranged for her to be transferred directly to our ward.

The term 'backstreet brigade' referred to one of the abortionists that carried out their work in the backstreets of Belfast. At that time therapeutic abortion was illegal in Northern Ireland and only permitted for rare medical conditions that endangered the life of the mother.

The aim of the abortionist was not always to empty the uterus of the pregnancy, but merely to start the process, so the woman could then legitimately go to hospital with signs and symptoms of impending miscarriage. ('Miscarriage,' was the lay term used for spontaneous early pregnancy loss. The medical word, 'abortion,' had connotations of illegal termination, and was not used with patients).

There were two main methods used by abortionists. The first involved pushing a long, thin object (usually a knitting needle) through the cervix (neck of the womb), to puncture the membranous sac surrounding the embryo and to dislodge it from the lower part of the uterus (womb). This would stimulate the uterus to contract, causing pain and bleeding – the early signs of miscarriage. The other technique was to inject a solution through the cervix with a douche nozzle, turkey baster or similar implement, to achieve the same disruption of the pregnancy. This solution was usually soap and water or a household disinfectant. The trouble with both of these methods was that part of their *modus operandi* was, in effect, to introduce infection into the uterus. The other risk with the knitting needle approach was, if pushed in too far, it would perforate the wall of the uterus and cause bleeding and infection within the main peritoneal cavity of the pelvis and abdomen – a potentially lethal complication.

With these thoughts in the background, I went to see the patient in question, Mary Conway, in the clinical room of the gynaecology ward where I could do a thorough pelvic examination.

I introduced myself. "Hello, Miss Conway (this was pre-Ms), I'm sorry for your troubles. Shall I call you Mary or Miss Conway?"

"Mary, is fine, Doctor."

"The doctor you saw in casualty thinks you're having a miscarriage. Did you know you were pregnant?"

"Yes, I did, I missed two of my monthlys."

Mary was a red-headed young women of medium build and with clear pale skin, although her cheeks were red with fever. Her social history was a bit unusual for that time. Most unmarried women of her age would still live at home with their parents. Mary, however, had achieved her independence and lived in a flat with two other young women. They all worked at a big tobacco factory in Belfast. She had a short-term relationship with a man, and they broke up before she knew she was pregnant. She had told no one in her family of the pregnancy.

The ward nurse was with me when I examined Mary. The bleeding from the cervix was light and there was no trauma to the vagina or cervix. So, no signs of a traumatic instrumental attempt at abortion. The uterus was enlarged to the size of a nine-week pregnancy, the slightest movement of which gave her severe pain. Even putting a small Q-tip gently into the cervix for bacterial culture, including possible gonorrhoea, was acutely tender. The examination confirmed the diagnosis of septic abortion – the problem was that nature had not yet provided the cure, which was to empty the uterus of its infected contents.

After the examination, the nurse returned to the ward. I could now try and broach the subject of our suspicion that Mary had used the services of a backstreet abortionist. We knew that some of them plied their trade in streets around the Royal – one of whom was rumoured to have some nursing experience.

The duty of the doctor in these cases was outlined in my 1962 copy of the eighteenth edition of *Pye's Surgical Handicraft* by Hamilton Bailey. This was listed as, "Being a Practical Guide for the House Surgeon" – something I was constantly in need of. The relevant passage was as follows: "There is little doubt that many abortions are induced by criminal action. If the patient herself is at fault, it is no part of the doctor's duty to report the matter to police, although the coroner must be informed should she die."

"Mary, you are having a miscarriage, but at the moment it is complicated by a serious infection around the pregnancy in your womb. We know when this happens there has sometimes been an attempt to start the miscarriage. Now, this is just between you and me, I won't write any of this in your medical record, it's completely confidential. But if there was any interference, I need to know, as it could be vital for your treatment. I don't need any details of who or where, just a bit about the how."

My reason for the 'how' was to try and find out if a knitting needle, or equivalent, had been used – if so, it could have perforated the uterus, as opposed to the douche soap fluid technique, which was less likely to penetrate the uterine wall. The relevance of this was related to the need to curette the uterus and empty its septic contents. If there had been a perforation, curettage would be more difficult and dangerous.

"I just remember she put her fingers far up inside me, and I think there was a plastic bag with fluid. It's hard to be sure, they gave me a lot of gin before, so I was a bit out of it."

So, probably no perforation. While this was a plus, the potential for serious complications was still high. The focus of dead, infected pregnancy tissue within the uterus would inevitably spread infection to adjacent structures in the pelvis, and ultimately lead to life-threatening pelvic and abdominal peritonitis. If untreated, Mary could descend into septic shock – a fatal condition in which the body's basic metabolic and circulatory functions collapse due to overwhelming infection.

By now, Mary Conway's clinical condition was unfolding, and she was showing all the bad symptoms and signs of septic abortion. She had continuous and worsening pelvic and abdominal pain. She was flushed and having episodes of rigors (shivering). Her pulse was a rapid 110, and her temperature remained high at 104 (We used Fahrenheit in the 1960s).

We moved her to a side room with a single bed. I put up an intravenous drip (IV) and started antibiotics through her IV. Her breathing became rapid and a bit of panic, and perhaps guilt, was setting in. "I'm just a stupid wee girl. Am I going to die, Doctor?"

"You are certainly not stupid, and it's not your fault. And dying is not allowed on this ward. It's against the rules and absolutely forbidden. I could lose my job."

My weak attempt at reassuring humour did bring forth a little smile.

"Seriously, Mary, you're going to be OK. You were right to come to the hospital early, so we can treat you and get you over this. But it will take a few days, and you will need a small operation to clear away the infected tissue in your womb."

It was time to get my senior registrar, Bertie Mason, involved. He reviewed everything we had done so far.

"Right," he said. "We need to flood her system with the antibiotics for two or three hours and then empty the uterus by D&C (Dilatation of the cervix and Curettage of the uterus). We'll do that together. I think she's on the verge of septic shock, so we can't hang about."

Bertie supervised me doing the D&C. This was usually a simple operation - but not in this case. Infection made the walls of the uterus soft and vulnerable to perforation by the curette, a complication which could result in the need to open her abdomen, and perhaps even necessitate hysterectomy – a catastrophic outcome in a nineteen-year-old. When I had finished, Bertie sat down and checked my work. He explored the uterine cavity and, to my chagrin, he found some tissue that I had missed due to my timid fear of perforating the uterus. Bertie was magnanimous.

"It's better to be gentle than aggressive in surgery," he said. "I just have more miles on the clock than you."

Mary's condition improved dramatically over the next twelve hours. Once again, the triumph of youth over medical adversity – along with some help from the health service. We did keep her in hospital for a full seven days of antibiotics. Her only visitors were her two flatmates. Mary Conway would live to fight another day.

*

In truth, the social milieu of that era did not serve young women well. Both the Catholic and Protestant religious authorities passed very harsh judgment on pre-marital sex. Indeed, some Protestant groups had a very dismal and restrictive view of life in general. Religious graffiti in both town and country was ubiquitous, and mostly negative. One of the more common messages, displayed on walls, barns or the sidewalls of houses was, "The Wages of Sin is Death." Another popular, and slightly more uplifting version was, "Jesus Saves." This, however, lent itself to alteration by the equally ubiquitous Ulster humourist, who added, "George Best Scores on the Rebound." (George Best was a legendary football (soccer) star from Belfast). The message, "In God We Trust," might provoke the addendum, "All Others Pay Cash."

In some ways the health service wasn't all that helpful. In the 1960s, the main focus of hospital contraception services was the provision of tubal ligation for women who had completed their families. Young women had limited options. Until 1967, within the National Health Service, the birth control pill could only be prescribed to married women. Family planning clinics were few and far between, and many GPs were not geared up to provide the full range of birth control services. Condoms could be bought, but you had to know where to get them.

Therapeutic abortion was governed by the Criminal Offences Against the Person Act of 1861. In essence, termination of pregnancy was only permitted for medical conditions that threatened the life of the mother. The penalty for both the recipient and the provider of illegal abortion was life imprisonment. In 1967, the British parliament passed the Abortion Act, which came into effect in April 1968. This act provided much more open access to therapeutic abortion. But the Act did not apply in Northern Ireland, where the more rigid Protestant groups were just as opposed to abortion as the Catholic Church. Thus, in the North of Ireland, the 1861 Act remained in effect. It would be more than fifty years, in 2019, before that act was repealed, and the women of Northern Ireland gained the same right to abortion services as their British counterparts. (In the 1990s, some two thousand women each year travelled from Northern Ireland to Britain for termination of pregnancy).

One of the side effects, noted in all countries after they provide accessible and safe abortion services, is that the incidence of 'spontaneous' septic abortion falls dramatically. Most of these cases were, in fact, the result of illegal attempts to induce abortion by desperate women, sometimes putting themselves at lethal risk – the Mary Conways of this world.

Chapter 21

The Firing Squad

In the 1960s about twenty percent of women in Belfast delivered their babies at home under the care of the district midwife service and general practitioners. When an acute complication arose, not unknown in obstetrics, the midwife or GP called the maternity hospital and asked for the Obstetric Flying Squad. Typical of Belfast humour the Flying Squad was known to the locals as the Firing Squad. As in: "She took that bad in her labour that they had to send for the firing squad." The ambulance was called from the depot in the hospital grounds and came to the front entrance of the Royal Maternity Hospital. The obstetric registrar, houseman or SHO, and a midwife collected the bundles containing instruments for delivery and operative obstetric procedures, as well as two units of O negative blood, which in those days came in bottles and was kept on the labour ward. (O negative was the universal blood donor group and could be given to anyone in an emergency). These three then joined the ambulance and left for the patient's home with suitable dispatch and loud siren noises en route.

One of the main reasons for a flying squad call was obstetric haemorrhage, and this was one of my first outings as an SHO. The senior registrar, me and a midwife went. It was to one of the small industrial row houses where Mrs. Bridie O'Mahony had just been delivered by the district midwife and was bleeding heavily. The cause of her bleeding was a retained placenta (afterbirth) which prevented the uterus (womb) muscle from contracting and stopping the blood loss. We all knew the midwife, Joan Davidson, who had just finished her midwifery training at the RMH and had recently started on the district.

"The delivery went beautifully," said Joan. "I gave her the usual injection of ergometrine," (a drug routinely given after delivery to contract the uterus, reduce bleeding and help deliver the placenta). "I had her lovely wee baby girl all cleaned and bundled up, when she started bleeding. I did a quick exam and the placenta was still trapped in the uterus. I gave another dose of ergometrine, but she kept bleeding so, that's when I called you – thank goodness for the flying squad, we're all alone out here."

One could only sympathise with her. Labour and delivery were grand when it went well. However, even in apparently normal cases it was the shortest stage of labour, the time between the birth of the baby and delivery of the placenta, that was by far the most dangerous for the mother. Just as applause and congratulations greet the safe delivery of the baby, danger lurks to threaten the mother. No midwife or obstetrician could ever relax until the placenta was safely delivered and the uterus well contracted to control bleeding. Things could go from triumph to tragedy in a few minutes, as it had in this case.

David, the senior registrar, quickly appraised the situation and took charge. "Right. We're going to have to give her an anaesthetic and remove the placenta quickly or she's going to bleed out. Tom, get the chloroform ready and set up an intravenous drip. Nurse, check that there are no open fires."

The bottle of chloroform also included a small amount of ether, the blend of the two agents was felt to be safer than one alone. The mixture was flammable and potentially explosive, hence the need to find and douse any adjacent open fires -- which was the common method of heating these homes.

I set up the IV and ran in saline solution as a prelude to the blood transfusion.

To remove the placenta David would have to put his hand into the uterus. Doing so would require an anaesthetic. In hospital this would have been given by a trained anaesthetist with modern techniques. In the home we had to revert to the old-fashioned mask with drops of the chloroform/ether mix on gauze - an outdated technique which I had never done. Anaesthetic agents are great but they all have potentially lethal side-effects; including chloroform, which I vaguely recalled could cause cardiac arrest and was one of the reasons it was no longer used – except on the Belfast Flying Squad by one inexperienced T.F. Baskett. After all, anaesthesia was a separate specialty for good reason and here was I about to give one with a bottle and gauze for the first time – not exactly a career-enhancing move.

"Let's get the placenta out, stop the bleeding and then we can give her a blood transfusion. We've got to get that placenta out now," said David, trying to hide the tension in his voice.

Our hospital midwife helped me by holding Mrs. O'Mahony's hand and making encouraging noises – at least they were encouraging to me.

I leaned over Mrs. O'Mahony and, with what I hoped was a confident tone, said: "We need to get your afterbirth out to stop the bleeding. To do that I have to give you a wee mask to breathe which will make you sleepy. We will look after you. Everything will be OK."

I meant what I said and hoped for both our sakes I wouldn't be proved a liar. Fortunately, Mrs. O'Mahony was pretty composed and trusting, not to mention weak from blood loss. Most patients in that era were trusting; they had grown up with the National Health Service, had a GP, as well as District Nurse and District Midwifery services. They assumed, correctly, that everyone in the system was there to help them. It made our work much easier and our desire to justify their trust even greater.

The Schimmelbusch mask, first used in 1890, was metal with an oval shape and had two semicircular strips to support the layer of gauze and keep it from touching the patient's face. I put chloroform/ether drops from the bottle on the gauze and placed the mask gently over her mouth and nose. I was so worried about the risks of chloroform that I hovered closely over the bottle and mask and almost anaesthetised myself from the vapours. She soon became relaxed enough for David to remove the placenta and we got the bleeding stopped. However, she had lost a lot of blood.

"Her blood pressure is seventy over nothing and her pulse 120," said the midwife.

These were bad numbers and, along with her pale clammy appearance, confirmed that she was in severe shock from the blood loss.

David, while relieved that the placenta was out and that the bleeding was controlled, said urgently: "OK, we have to get blood started before we can transport her to hospital."

The bottles of blood were in the insulated box and were cold, having come from the fridge on the labour floor. We needed to warm it before transfusion. This was done by running the blood through coiled tubing placed in a basin of warm water; not too warm or the blood would be haemolyzed and unsafe for transfusion. Without a thermometer, a practical technique was what I called the Baby Bathwater Elbow Sensitivity Test (BBEST). You tested the water in the basin with your elbow, just as you would check that bathwater was not too hot for a baby. Fortunately, the IV was working well and the blood flowed smoothly. As a recent father, I was pleased to perform the elbow sensitivity test with the confidence of a qualified baby-bather.

The architecture of the upstairs of these most basic houses made transfer difficult. From the door off the street the narrow staircase went straight up and then turned sharply into the only bedroom. Through a wide opening on one side of the bedroom was an area about six feet deep that ran the whole length of the room – rather like a large open closet. On the floor of this area were mattresses on which all the children slept. It was not possible to have a rigid stretcher and manoeuvre it round the sharp corners. Thus, we moved the patient from her bedroom on a canvas stretcher with handles that allowed us to bend her round the corners. Our hospital midwife carried the bundled baby down after us. The district midwife stayed behind to clean up and get her equipment together.

The neighbours inevitably gathered around the ambulance as we left with the patient: a mixture of nosiness, concern, and a desire to help. They always closed ranks for one of their own.

"God love her, they had to get the firing squad."

"Don't you worry, Bridie, you'll be in good hands at the Royal."

"We'll look after your man and the children."

With these encouraging words ringing in our ears, we closed the back doors of the ambulance and returned to the RMH.

"Well done troops, another obstetric triumph – change of underwear all round!"

(Gallows humour was common and could be therapeutic when under stress. It can seem callous to the outsider and is really only understood by those on the frontline.)

*

Speaking of gallows humour. There was a joke around that time which became one of our standards, as follows: (To get the full effect it should be told with an exaggerated French accent.)

On the eve of the Battle of Waterloo, Napoleon Bonaparte and his valet, Pierre, were talking:

"Why is it, Pierre, that the Duke of Wellington always wears a scarlet tunic when he leads his men into battle?"

"I believe, Mon Emperor, it is in case he is wounded, so that the blood will not show and perhaps demoralise his soldiers."

"For tomorrow, Pierre, lay out my brown trousers."

Thus, in our group of like-minded, slightly paediatric gallows humourists, 'brown trouser time', became the catch phrase for moments of adversity as we progressed through medical school and life as junior doctors.

Chapter 22
Fetal Distress

It was rare to get much sleep when on obstetric night call at the Royal Maternity Hospital. In recognition of this, the administrative hierarchy provided bread, butter, eggs and baked beans in the labour ward kitchen for the makings of a late supper for junior medical staff. This was essential as fuel to get you through the night. You cooked the eggs to your own recipe on the gas stove, but lots of bread and butter were always involved. Two fried eggs in a triple-decker sandwich was my specialty.

About midnight during one such meal a call came through for the flying squad. I now had about eighteen months obstetrical experience, so the senior resident told me to go with the houseman (intern) and midwife. This was a mark of his confidence in me, so I was pleased to be given the responsibility.

The call came from the district midwife. She was dealing with a patient who, with her risk factors, should have been booked for hospital delivery. However, thirty-nine-year-old Mrs. Maeve Cooney had refused and chosen to deliver at home – after all, as she saw it, she had delivered eight children before without mishap.

We only had a brief message from the midwife who had called from a public phone box in the street outside the house, before quickly returning to look after her patient. Mrs. Cooney's labour had started normally, but now she was bleeding more than usual with continuous lower abdominal pain, even between contractions. The midwife said "The fetal heart is all over the place, up and down .... Things are not right .... I don't like the look of her." We were to, "Come quickly."

The normal fetal heart rate (FHR) is between 110 and 160 beats per minute, so "up and down" presumably meant less than 110 at times and more than 160 at other times – a possible sign of reduced oxygen supply to the fetus. This was before the invention of portable hand-held ultrasound FHR monitors, so the fetal heart was listened to with a small cylindrical fetal stethoscope applied to the mother's abdomen. You leaned over, put your ear on the other end of the stethoscope and counted the FHR timing it with the second hand of your watch. This could be difficult in a mother moving about with the pain of labour. However, with practice you got quite good at it and mothers always tried to cooperate when you were checking on the welfare of their baby.

The houseman, Andrew McCartney, was a good friend, two years junior to me at Queen's Medical School, and just starting his obstetric training. Our hospital midwife was the very experienced Beth O'Neill. Off we went in the ambulance to the house, two miles away in North Belfast. Because of the worrying FHR I told the ambulance driver not to delay. The traffic was light at this time of night, so only intermittent siren warnings were needed to speed us along.

We found our patient in a terrace of small houses, one step up from the two-up, two-down industrial working-class model, but still a fairly modest three-up, three-down job. Mild mayhem greeted us. Behind a retinue of female neighbours and children (no men in sight), we discovered Mrs. Cooney and the district midwife, Janet Smith, in an upstairs bedroom.

"Right," I said to our midwife, Beth. "Clear this lot away – everyone out of the house except us."

Mrs. Cooney was writhing on the bed, very distressed with continuous pain. There was more than the usual loss of blood, but not an unduly worrying amount. She was one of those small thin women who look weak and wretched, but are often remarkably tough and resilient – now, however, she was frightened and at the end of her tether.

The district midwife was worried. "The fetal heart has been low since I called you – it's between 60 and 100. She's fully dilated but the head won't budge, even though she's pushing well."

"Mrs. Cooney, I'm Dr. Baskett from the Royal Maternity and I need to check you, so we can help your wee one into the world."

"Jesus, Mary and Joseph …. God help me. This is different from the others, Doctor …. There's too much pain …. All the time …. It's not right, so it's not …. Something's wrong …. What about my baby?"

Janet Smith, her midwife, consoled and encouraged the patient while I examined her abdomen. Even without a contraction, her lower uterus was very tender. It felt like a big baby – probably the reason Mrs. Cooney was having trouble with the delivery. I checked the fetal heart rate (FHR), I only needed a few seconds to tell that it was about fifty to sixty beats per minute – far too slow. So, the combination of continuous pain, a tender uterus, bleeding and a slow heart rate added up to separation of part of the placenta – the baby's oxygen-providing lifeline. As the district midwife had recorded a persistently slow FHR for the last ten to fifteen minutes, this was a fetus under extreme stress from reduced oxygen supply.

I quickly put on sterile gloves and checked the position of the fetal head, which was nice and low in her pelvis. There are landmarks on the skull that can tell you which way the baby's head is facing. This is essential information if you are to apply forceps safely and accelerate delivery of the baby – which I needed to do as quickly as possible. A fetal heart rate of sixty may suddenly plunge to zero and the baby can die in a few minutes.

I could tell from the skull bone edges that the head was in the favourable, face down (occipito-anterior) position – sometimes nature does the right thing and helps you out. I would be able to deliver her easily with forceps. Thank goodness for the experienced Beth O'Neill, who already had all the instruments and kit we needed laid out on the end of the bed.

"OK, Mrs. Cooney, your baby's heart rate is a bit slow, so we need to get him delivered as soon as possible. I will use forceps, but you have done very well, and the delivery should be easy. But we must do it now. Please do exactly as we tell you, and everything will be alright."

"Andrew and Beth, each of you hold her legs, while I put on the forceps."

With each of them on opposite sides of the bed holding her legs, I leaned over and was able to slip the forceps blades on either side of the fetal head. Not for the first time, I was hugely impressed and grateful for the courage and cooperation that many women *in extremis* were able to muster.

"Mrs. Cooney, the forceps are now cradling the baby's head, so if you push, we can deliver him."

It was a simple easy delivery with one push from her and a little pull from me. Just as well, as my twisted and leaning across the bottom of the bed was not conducive to advanced technical manoeuvres.

The baby, a girl, later to be named Mary, was pale, not breathing, and limp – now for the serious part. She had been born through meconium (fetal bowel content) – meaning her fetal bowel movement during labour mixed the meconium with the amniotic fluid. This could be normal, but it can also be a sign of fetal distress due to reduced oxygen supply – which it obviously was in this case. Meconium is a thick, tenacious substance which, if inhaled during the baby's first breath, can cause serious, even fatal, lung inflammation. In the 1960s we did not have neonatal intensive care units with ventilators, so even relatively mild cases of meconium aspiration could be lethal.

Beth immediately handed me the mucus aspirator. This consisted of a central small bottle to trap the mucus or meconium. Connected to one side of the trap was narrow tubing, the end of which you placed in the baby's mouth and throat. A second tube came from the other side of the trap and was equipped with a mouthpiece that you sucked on. Thus, you aspirated the meconium, which was contained in the trap, blocking its suction into your mouth. I was able to suck and aspirate most of the meconium out before the baby's first breath; not that she was quick to take her first breath.

After the suction I used an Ambu bag* to squeeze air into her lungs, but she still did not breathe on her own. Beth used a small infant stethoscope to listen to the baby's heart rate and breath sounds as I pumped air into the lungs. At first, she could not hear any heartbeat, but within thirty seconds she detected a slow rate of forty to sixty, rising quickly to the normal rate over one hundred. Three minutes after her birth, Mary was breathing on her own and pinking up nicely. By five minutes she was expressing some welcome cries of righteous indignation.

Janet Smith, looked after Mrs. Cooney and delivered the placenta without incident – about a quarter of the placental surface had blood clot stuck to it, confirming that it had separated before delivery and explaining the reduced oxygen supply to the baby. There were no lacerations or excess bleeding, and Mrs. Cooney was mightily relieved.

"Thank youse all, and God love you."

"I'm afraid we are going to have to take you into the Royal, Mrs. Cooney, mostly to keep an eye on your wee girl. She seems fine now but will need close observation for a day or two. Your midwife, Janet, will arrange for the neighbours to look after your other children."

Andrew McCartney had mostly been a spectator but would have learned a lot on his first trip out with the flying squad.

The Ambu bag was invented by the Danish anaesthetist, Henning Rubin, in 1957. It is the most commonly used hand-held resuscitator, consisting of a face mask attached to a flexible air bag. Once the face mask is applied and sealed over the patient's mouth and nose the air bag is squeezed forcing air into the lungs. When the pressure on the bag is released it reinflates from the other end. A valve between the mask and the bag, allows the patient's lungs to deflate to the outside air and not back into the bag. The face mask comes in three sizes – the smallest of which is the one used on infants, as in this case.

"Good save, Baskett," he said, "Where the hell did you learn neonatal resuscitation?"

"All part of the highly skilled, multi-talented and superior junior doctor profile – skills which, by the way, you should acquire without delay."

"You're full of it, Baskett."

"Aren't we all, old hand, aren't we all?"

Baby Mary did well, and Mrs. Cooney had a couple of days rest in hospital. I would like to record that she took up our offer of postpartum tubal ligation, but she didn't. Although I'm pretty sure she'd had enough of the 'gifts from God,' as each pregnancy was defined by the church.

Chapter 23

She's Having a Fit

It was a busy evening in the Royal Maternity Hospital when the request came through for the flying squad. The senior registrar, Bertie Mason, was tied up with a complex set of twins so, as the SHO next in line, I took the call. It was Sam Gibson, a general practitioner with a large domiciliary obstetric practice.

"It's Kathy Ryan, she's having a fit and I need the squad."

"Is she in labour?" I asked.

"No, she's been away at her mother's and missed her last two clinic visits. She's gone eclamptic on us."

"We're on our way," I said, after getting the address.

The twins were late on in labour, and as this was not a case for the inexperienced, Bertie Mason would have to stay and see them safely delivered.

"Right, Tom," he said. "You have to go. Take the midwife and a student with you. Brew up the Avertin and bring the patient in."

The patient, Kathy Ryan, and her husband, Des, were known to many of the junior staff at the hospital. They were a lovely couple who had been through the medical mill with prolonged infertility. They both held clerking jobs in an insurance company office and had married later in life than usual – she was twenty-nine and he, thirty-one years old. Having endured their unexplained inability to get pregnant for almost a decade they had, to their surprise and delight, finally achieved this when Kathy Ryan was thirty-eight years old. We shared their joy when the pregnancy was confirmed.

She was booked for delivery at the RMH and attended our hospital's antenatal clinic. Kathy Ryan was now thirty-six weeks pregnant, but her last visit to the clinic was three weeks ago. She had missed her last two appointments because, as an only child, she had gone to look after her sick mother in Ballymena – a town about thirty-five miles (55km) from Belfast. Upon her return home that afternoon her husband had noticed her face and feet had become swollen. In the early evening she complained of a persistent headache and said that her vision was 'fading in and out.' Des Ryan called her doctor, Sam Gibson, who had been her GP since she was a teenager. He came to their house at once and found her resting in bed. On taking her blood pressure (BP) he noted it to be very high: 190 over 120. Just as he finished taking her BP, she had a grand mal seizure (a major epileptic-type fit: in the 1960s we used the word 'fit' for what is now called a 'seizure'). Doctor Gibson protected her as best he could during the attack, which lasted less than a minute. Fortunately, the Ryan house had a phone, so he was able to call for the flying squad without delay.

Eclampsia is a rare and potentially lethal condition peculiar to pregnancy. The dramatic presentation is the eclamptic fit, associated with high blood pressure that can develop in late pregnancy. There is also a risk of cerebral haemorrhage (bleed into the brain) and death, as well as serious dysfunction of other organs, including the kidneys, heart and liver. It is rare because, with regular antenatal care, its predecessor, pre-eclampsia, can be recognised and treated before eclampsia develops. In Mrs. Ryan's case her three-week hiatus from antenatal care, in order to look after her mother, had led to the warning signs of pre-eclampsia being missed.

The role of the flying squad in cases of eclampsia was to prevent further fits and get the woman safely to hospital. The treatment we used was a very strong sedative called Avertin (tribromethol). It was given rectally as an enema. Avertin had to be prepared by making a weak solution from a concentrate heated in water. A thermometer was used as the drug was temperature-sensitive and required testing with a dye (congo red) to rule out toxic degradation. We brewed this up on the labour ward gas stove and put the prepared solution in a thermos flask: 38-39^0C being the ideal temperature for rectal administration.

I had the Avertin cooked and ready by the time the flying squad ambulance arrived at the front entrance of the hospital. This was a case for both full speed and full siren from the ambulance driver as we sped to the house, about two miles from the RMH. It was essential to try and prevent further fits, as each episode was potentially lethal to the mother and her baby.

Doctor Gibson was in the upstairs bedroom with Kathy Ryan when we arrived; he was a seasoned campaigner in the world of GP obstetrics, but he had not seen a case of eclampsia before – and he was rattled. As a neophyte obstetrician I had only seen one eclamptic and she bled into her brain and her baby had died before delivery. Kathy Ryan was semi-conscious and lying in the semi-prone position in bed. Doctor Gibson had sensibly placed her in this posture to prevent her choking on her tongue or from aspirating mucus or vomitus into her lungs.

An eclamptic fit is distressing to behold. It is usually preceded by a fixed stare and twitching of the facial muscles. All the muscles of the body go into a tonic spasm followed by a clonic phase of alternate contraction and relaxation. During this convulsive clonic phase, the jaw muscles may bite and badly damage the tongue, so a mouth gag is needed for protection. Doctor Gibson had used the first thing he had to hand for this purpose – his tobacco pipe. Such was the strength of her convulsive teeth-gnashing that Mrs. Ryan had broken through the stem of the pipe.

I quickly got the enema rubber tubing and funnel ready to administer the Avertin. Mrs. Ryan was beginning to stir and her facial muscles were twitching, so another fit was imminent. I inserted the rectal tube, poured the Avertin from the thermos flask into the funnel and held it high to speed the drug into her rectum. Not exactly high-tech, but remarkably effective. Within a few minutes Kathy Ryan was deeply sedated and snoring nicely. It would now be safe to move her to hospital. We kept her in the semi-prone position and carried her downstairs on a flexible canvas stretcher – the necessary extra muscle being provided by the medical student.

Mrs. Ryan's husband, Des, had hovered anxiously throughout. I had met him before and I now explained what we were doing. Understandably, he was distraught, but in control; he could tell from everyone's demeanour how serious things were. He didn't have a car, so I broke the rules and allowed him to come with us in the ambulance back to the hospital.

Having got her safely back to the RMH we were able to control her blood pressure and prevent further convulsions with intravenous drugs. Within two hours we had her stabilised and the heart rate of the baby was normal. She was now sedated but conscious and, happily, there were no signs of neurological damage.

It is an obstetric truism that eclampsia can only be cured by delivering the baby and ending the pregnancy. If it is simple and likely to succeed within a few hours, induction of labour may be chosen – if not, caesarean delivery is considered. I examined Mrs. Ryan and her cervix was firmly closed and very unfavourable for induction, which would almost certainly fail. Add to this her age and the long period of infertility, and both Bertie and I agreed that caesarean delivery would be best. The problem was that permission to carry out a caesarean section was the one situation where even the senior registrar had to get agreement from the consultant on call. This was usually straightforward, and in the three years I was at the RMH I never saw one of the senior consultants come in at night. The one exception was a junior consultant who was revered by the junior medical and midwifery staff.

Unfortunately for us, Dr Henderson, one of the most senior consultants was on call that night. He was an old school conservative obstetrician who still held to the principle of 'stabilising' the eclamptic patient for 24-48 hours before attempting to deliver the baby. In fact, this long period of 'stabilisation' just meant watching and waiting while the patient and her baby deteriorated. The modern medical view was to avoid this delay – but Dr. Henderson was not modern.

Bertie and I were going to have to come up with a plan to convince him, over the phone, that Mrs. Ryan warranted caesarean delivery.

"I know him, and eclampsia isn't enough." Bertie said. "He'll try and get us to delay overnight. Even with her age and infertility, we need more."

"OK," I said. "What if we say it's a breech?"

"But it isn't."

"He doesn't know that, and if he found out, which he won't because he's never in the hospital, you can say it was that idiot, Baskett, who doesn't know his arse from his elbow – or in this case the fetal arse from the fetal head."

"That might work, but he could still stall us off,"

"Let's add a bit of fetal distress," I said (Fetal distress being a sign that the baby may not be getting enough oxygen). "You could tell him the fetal heart has fallen to less than 100 on four occasions in the last hour, and you're worried her convulsions may have damaged the placenta and caused it to partially separate."

"You should take up writing fiction, Tom."

"It's deceitful, but we both know it's the best decision for her, and especially for her baby." I was really getting into it now. I was annoyed that this woman's chance, and probably her only chance, of having a healthy baby could be thwarted by an arbitrary veto given over the phone. Given, at that, by a consultant who had not even attended his own hospital antenatal clinic for the last eleven years.

Bertie was a kind and gentle soul, but very much aware of the negative effect a senior consultant could have on his career.

"The only way you're going to sound convincing," I said, "Is if you're convinced, she is a thirty-eight-year-old eclamptic, with ten years infertility, a breech presentation and developing fetal distress. Bloody hell, Bertie, even Hippocrates would grant her a caesarean delivery for that lot."

And he did – Henderson that is, not Hippocrates.

At about two a.m. we delivered Kathy Ryan of a healthy baby boy to be called, appropriately, Desmond. At the caesarean section there was thick meconium (fetal bowel content) – often a sign of fetal distress. There was also partial separation of the placenta. So, clear evidence that delay could have been disastrous for young Desmond.

"Good call, Baskett," I said.

"You're a chancer, Baskett, but in this case, you were dead on. Thanks for being so creatively devious and stubborn."

"No probs."

It was one of those cases when everything could have gone wrong for the mother and baby. I was relieved and proud at the good outcome, and choked up to see the deserving parents so happy. One of those nuggets that sustains you through the sometimes mundane drudgery of clinical medicine.

*

Obstetric flying squads started in Britain in the 1930s when most maternity cases were managed at home by midwives and GPs. The Belfast flying squad was started in 1943. By the 1980s, as the number of home births diminished, and as the speed and sophistication of the ambulance service improved, the relevance and need for the obstetric flying squad disappeared.

Chapter 24
Beyond Futterly

At the end of my houseman's year, I decided to specialise in surgery. This would entail passing a major examination to become a fellow of the Royal College of Surgeons – of which there were four: Edinburgh, England, Glasgow, and Ireland. Common to all colleges was a preliminary primary fellowship exam which had a failure rate of eighty per cent plus. It covered, in fearsome detail, the subjects of anatomy, physiology and pathology as applied to surgery. The best way to pass this exam was to get one of the coveted, but low paid jobs as a demonstrator in anatomy and physiology at the university, teaching pre-clinical medical students. This also allowed time to do a lot of locum work as a general practitioner, to augment the low salary. I did this and managed to pass the primary exam at the Royal College of Surgeons in Dublin, in June 1966.

During our clinical jobs as junior doctors there was no guided preparation for the specialty exams and no formal postgraduate teaching whatsoever. Self-directed learning is often touted as a modern educational concept – rubbish – we were doing it before we or they knew what it was; we were entirely on our own. You talked to those who had gone before and tried to carve out study time from a busy day, and often night, clinical job. We did not read journals, we used text-books. The best preparation was to take tutorials for the medical students, which forced you to organise the topic. I did a lot of this. In addition, because of our heavy clinical load, we were pretty knowledgeable about how to recognise and manage most conditions in our speciality.

In March 1969 I attempted my first full fellowship exam. I had changed from surgery to obstetrics and gynaecology (O&G). The Edinburgh Royal College had a combined General Surgery and O&G exam. The written essay exams were held over two days at the end of one week followed a few days later by the clinicals and orals.

I turned up for my first clinical exam at the Edinburgh Royal Infirmary on the Tuesday morning in one of the old circular wards with about twelve beds around the periphery. In the centre of the ward, under a single hanging light bulb was my examiner, Professor Cameron. He was very senior and looked amiable but absent minded – in keeping with his rank.

"What's your name, Doctor?" he said.

"Baskett, sir."

"Ah, yes, I have you here," he scrutinised his sheet of paper, with the candidates' names on it. "Where are you from, although I think I can tell from your accent?" he said kindly.

"Belfast, sir."

"Right," he said, holding up an X-ray film under the electric light bulb. "Have a look at this man's chest X-ray. There he is over there." He pointed to a man across the ward – who was in his forties, with a stomach tube down his nose, and had an intravenous drip in place. He looked a bit sore and sorry for himself. "This chap came in two nights ago with acute abdominal pain and ended up having an operation for it. Here's his chest X-ray, tell me what you make of it?"

I took the X-ray and held it up against the overhead light bulb. On our ward rounds at home, we were often asked to look at X-rays, which many consultants insisted be kept at the end of each patient's bed. There was a certain ritual involved; this included checking the name of the patient and the right and left orientation – there was an R or L marker on each film. As I looked at this film there was a L marker, but the heart, which normally lies to the left of the chest was, in this case pointing right. Thus, assuming the marker was correct, this man had *dextrocardia* (right-sided heart). In itself, although rare, this was not remarkable, and his heart function would be normal. However, dextrocardia was often associated with a similar inversion of the abdominal organs, so-called *situs inversus*. If so, this meant that the appendix would be on his left side, rather than its usual position on the right. Appendicitis was a common cause of emergency admission with abdominal pain, and if that were the case in this man his pain would have been on the left, creating a diagnostic conundrum. The surgeon would have considered other causes for his pain and probably made a bigger abdominal incision, before finding the inflamed appendix on the left.

I outlined all this to Professor Cameron, emphasising that this was predicated (I popped in this impressive word for good measure) on the L marker being correctly placed by the X-ray technician. A look of surprise and delight came over his face. "Absolutely right," he said. "That's exactly what happened. Well done. What did you say your name was?"

"Baskett, sir, B-a-s-k-e-t-t, Baskett from Belfast, sir." He was a kindly man, but a bit bumbling and forgetful. I wanted to be sure that my diagnostic triumph was correctly attributed to me and not some other candidate on his list, which he was waving around a bit too casually for my liking.

"You know, no one else got that one this morning, I thought we had you all stumped."

"Thank you, sir, Baskett, on your list there I think, sir," I said, pointing to my name on his paper.

This was the sporting equivalent of serving four straight aces in the final game of the fifth set at Wimbledon, or diving over for the winning try for Ireland in the rugby football, triple-crown decider. 'Hitting it out of the park,' in American terminology.

The rest of my clinical exam with Professor Cameron went well, he was almost answering his own questions, he was so impressed. One of those rare times that you can't lose. Thank goodness for our bedside training ritual with X-rays.

Indeed, the rest of the day's clinicals and orals went on in the same vein. In boxing parlance – they never laid a glove on me. I couldn't put a foot wrong – no futterly this time. My only discomfort was that I had bought a new white shirt for the occasion and the collar was so firmly starched that my neck was rubbed raw and oozing blood by the end of the day.

The tradition in Edinburgh was that at the end of the day's clinicals and orals, the examiners would meet and decide, pass or fail, for each candidate. The odds were that sixty to seventy percent of us would fail. At about six p.m. a secretary opened the college door, outside which the more hopeful candidates had congregated. The door opened onto a busy city street, so we stood there in the light rain as the public walked by.

The secretary held up a paper in her hands and said, "I will read out the examination numbers of the successful candidates. If your number is called, you may step past me into the college and join the examiners for sherry. Number six, number eleven" …. Yes, that's me, good old number eleven – not eleven per cent, I hasten to add. Damp, but triumphant, I strode into the college. About six of us joined the examiners for some pretty execrable, cheap, but hugely welcome sherry. Professor Cameron gave me a large smile and a conspiratorial nod. The examiners congratulated each of us, addressing us as, Mister – the title accorded to surgeons. In the United Kingdom the use of 'Mister' to denote a qualified surgeon was rooted in the historical evolution of the specialty from the original barber-surgeons, who had no university degree and were not entitled to be called doctor. It took me six years to acquire 'Doctor,' and only five years to revert to 'Mister.' But in the hospital rankings it was a step up.

I sat the fellowship exam of the Royal College of Obstetricians and Gynaecologists three months later, in June 1969. In my oral, held at the college in London, there were two examiners: one northern Englishman and the other, a woman obstetrician from one of the big London teaching hospitals. The Englishman did the usual decent thing of trying to put the candidate at ease at the start of the oral.

"What's the tie you're wearing, Doctor?"

"Staff tie of The Royal Victoria Hospital, Belfast, sir."

At which the snooty, plum-in-mouth Londoner, turned to him and said, "Oh, I didn't know they wore ties over there."

It was the classic, put the provincials in their place, approach of the entitled and insecure. The 1960s was a time when all the advances in O&G were being made in regional hospitals outside London. They were so busy feeling superior and chasing private practice, that they didn't know how far behind they were.

I took my last exam in 1997, forty-five years after my first ill-fated eleven per cent in Arithmetic. I had, during a sabbatical in 1994-95, done the history of medicine course at the Worshipful Society of Apothecaries of London. The examination for the diploma consisted of a dissertation, one full day of essay questions, a twenty-minute lecture and an oral. I wrote the essays in the official examination room at Apothecaries Hall.

During my sabbatical I did some research on the romantic poet, John Keats, who lived and worked near where I was staying in London. Keats served as an apothecary's apprentice and sat the licensing exam at Apothecaries Hall in 1816. I discovered that he would have sat the papers, which he passed, in the same room. So, I took my exam in the room where one of my heroes from *A Pageant of English Verse* had sat his, almost 200 years before. As the young are prone to say, "How cool was that?"

For the first time in my long exam-taking career I actually won two prizes at this exam.

Goodbye to all futterly.

Chapter 25
The Pope Rules

In my last six months with the NHS, I was a registrar in the Northern Ireland system and assigned to country relief. I now had my postgraduate specialist qualifications in obstetrics and gynaecology and was able to cover up to and including consultant duties. Country relief, as the name implied, meant covering registrars or consultants in smaller hospitals when the local staff were sick or on holiday. I was based in Belfast and given notice, sometimes less then 24 hours, to go to one of the country hospitals for anywhere from a few days to three weeks. On occasion the registrar and consultant's holidays overlapped, so you did both junior doctor and consultant duties. Accommodation was in the doctors' quarters of the local hospital or, if that was unavailable, at the local hotel. Meals were taken in the hospital cafeteria. You were on duty all the time. I travelled to these hospitals by bus, so I had no local transport.

With a wife and two-year-old son this was a disrupting rotation, but it also provided great independent responsibility and clinical experience. As a result, I gained considerable clinical and surgical confidence. In one hospital I also came up against the might of the Catholic Church in the clinical arena.

As junior doctors in the Royal Maternity Hospital we served the local population from one of the surrounding Catholic districts of Belfast. We were familiar with the control exerted by the Catholic Church on the reproductive lives of its female adherents. This was manifest by a ban on any effective form of contraception, leading to unlimited fertility and large families – often exceeding ten children.

In the hospital antenatal clinic, we would broach the subject with the women and offer tubal ligation (sterilisation) on the day after their baby was born. Many would jump at the chance and expressed their desperation to try and limit their family size. Some wanted their priest's permission and we would present the compelling medical reasons why more pregnancies were a risk to their health. Many of these women had six to ten children and lived in the small row houses with two bedrooms and very basic amenities. Some priests were sympathetic and would allow the women to make her decision as a 'matter of conscience.' I remember one young priest who was particularly supportive of women in this situation. Unfortunately, he didn't last long and was reassigned to a remote rural area – presumably to reassess his attitude to the Church's teaching.

If a Catholic woman did decide to have a tubal ligation after her baby was born there were practicalities to be considered. Some of the Catholic midwives felt it was their duty to inform the priest if a woman was going to commit the 'grave sin' of contraception. She would inform the hospital priest, who would come in and warn the woman of the spiritual sequelae of committing such a sin; most women would buckle under this ecclesiastical pressure and cancel the operation. Thus, when we got the signed consent form, we kept it in the junior doctor's sitting room, rather than putting it on the patient's chart, where it might alert a vigilant informing midwife. When the woman delivered her baby, we would tell the non-Catholic sister on the labour ward; she would then arrange for non-Catholic midwives to be involved in the preparation for and performance of the tubal ligation. It was the only practical way to avoid church intervention in the woman's decision and to avoid embarrassment of the staff. This was easier than it sounds, everyone knew who was Catholic, and who was not.

I was covering both the registrar and consultant at a hospital in one of the more remote parts of Ulster when I first met Mrs. Colleen McGinty. She had been admitted to the antenatal ward by my predecessor because of chronic kidney disease and high blood pressure. This was her sixth full term pregnancy. She was thirty-four years old but looked at least ten years older. That said, she was a strikingly handsome woman with thick auburn hair and green eyes. Her previous five babies had all been delivered by caesarean section. When I inherited her, she was thirty-six weeks pregnant (forty weeks being full term). The plan was to get her to thirty-seven weeks, if her blood pressure didn't rise too high, and deliver her by repeat caesarean section.

After seeing her for a day or two I brought up the topic of birth control by sterilisation. From her chart I could see that her religion was listed as Catholic.

"Mrs. McGinty, what are your thoughts about pregnancy after this one?"

"Och, no more, Doctor, I don't think my health could stand it."

"I agree, and there are very good medical reasons to support that. When I do your caesarean section, it would be simple to tie your tubes at the same time. It won't add any risk to the operation or change your recovery time." I went over the technical details of tubal ligation.

"That would be great, Doctor, I just can't have any more children. But I'm Catholic, so my priest would have to agree."

"I don't think that would be a problem," I said, naively as it turned out. "You have compelling medical reasons with your kidney problem, blood pressure and, what will be your sixth caesarean section. Any one of these would be strong medical grounds, so I think the priest would agree. If you want, I could meet and go over this with him."

"Oh, yes please, Doctor. If you could, that would be grand. And I know my Kevin would be relieved, he feels bad enough getting me pregnant this time. The trouble is we're too fond of each other – he just has to look at me and I get pregnant." She smiled.

"OK then, you get in touch with your priest and I'll meet him. I'm here all the time, but late in the afternoon would be best for me."

My reason for optimism was the slight relaxation in the attitude toward birth control from some priests in the mid 1960s. If there were genuine medical grounds, and there certainly were in Mrs. McGinty's case, many priests were softening the church's position and allowing their supplicants to decide for themselves – as a matter of 'personal conscience.' It was a time when the contraceptive pill was being used more frequently. It could not be given for contraception in Catholic women, but it was often prescribed for 'menstrual problems'; and it was under this camouflage that many doctors prescribed the pill for their patients. In Mrs. McGinty's case, of course, the pill could not be given because of her kidney disease and high blood pressure.

In large part because of the pill, the church had established a Papal Commission in 1963 to review its position on contraception, and it was anticipated that it would soften its stance. Hopes were dashed, however, in July 1968, when Pope Paul V1 released *Humanae Vitae* - his hardline encyclical against birth control.

I met Father Muldoon on the Friday afternoon. Mrs. McGinty's caesarean delivery was booked for the next Monday. Our encounter went like this:

"Hello, Father, thank you for coming in for Mrs. McGinty."

"That's alright, I was here to see another patient."

Father Muldoon was in his late fifties, overweight and with nicotine-stained index and middle fingers on his right hand – a heavy smoker who ate well. He sat with his arms crossed and presented a defensive, unfriendly aura. He had met with Mrs. McGinty and knew why I was here.

"As you know, Father, Mrs. McGinty has been in hospital with her kidney disease and high blood pressure. She's due to have her sixth caesarean section on Monday. I'm here to provide any medical information you need to support her decision to have her tubes tied at the time of that caesarean delivery."

"I can't support that, Doctor."

"I know it's a big decision, but I can honestly say that her medical condition is such that another pregnancy would definitely shorten her life."

"That's in the hands of the Lord."

"It may be, but we have to deal with the medical complications that the Lord puts before us. By preventing another pregnancy, we have the best chance for Mrs. McGinty to stay alive and look after her six children."

"I can't sanction sterilisation."

"All she needs is for you to say it's a matter for her own conscience. You don't have to sanction it, just give her a chance to do what is best for her family. Personal conscience, that's all she needs, can't you give her that?"

"I'm sorry, but the church's ruling is quite clear on this."

"Isn't it supposed to be a merciful church? What part does mercy play in your decision?"

I was losing the battle. He wouldn't look me in the eye. I could see he wasn't going to budge, but I was going to go down fighting. "Father, I'm not a Catholic, but I can assure you that I am not exaggerating Mrs. McGinty's medical risks. Basically, your decision condemns her to an earlier grave than necessary and would leave her six children without a mother. How does the church feel about that?"

Laying it on a bit thick, Baskett, but essentially true.

"I don't make the rules, Doctor, but I know them, and the Pope has recently clarified this."

We continued to spar for a while, but that was it – *Humanae Vitae* trumped mercy and common sense. Father Muldoon was definitely from the 'Pray, Pay, and Obey' school of Catholicism and quite unmovable.

I held on to the forlorn hope that he might soften over the weekend, but of course he didn't.

After my session with the priest, I went to see Mrs. McGinty. She was crying quietly. Having been visited by Father Muldoon earlier, she knew the outcome.

"I'm very sorry, Mrs. McGinty, but I just couldn't convince your priest. To be honest with you I thought he was quite unreasonable."

"I know, Doctor, but without the church's blessing I can't go through with it. Thank you for doing your best with Father Muldoon, he can be a bit severe at times."

"You know, Mrs. McGinty, sometimes after so many caesarean sections there can be adhesions and scar tissue around the tubes. I will check for this on Monday when I do your section. If there is scarring it can act like a tubal ligation, block the tubes, and prevent future pregnancy. Perhaps its nature's way of dealing with things."

"Let's hope so, Doctor. I'll pray that it is, so."

"Thanks, I need all the help I can get from above, but I won't be relying on Father Muldoon to provide it."

She smiled. "You don't think much of him, do you?"

"No, I don't. I wouldn't give him the time of day."

I did her caesarean section on Monday morning and delivered her of a healthy wee baby girl – bringing her family to an evenly balanced boy-girl count of three each. When I checked her tubes, I was pleased to find scar tissue that looked as though they might become blocked. It took a great deal of surgical manipulation of the tubes to be certain. One has to be careful, however, as excessive surgical manipulation in and of itself can contribute to scar formation. But after careful appraisal, I did encounter enough scarring to suggest that another pregnancy was very unlikely.

Perhaps the Lord's guiding hand worked in her favour after all – in spite of Father Muldoon.

I encountered another, almost whimsical example of the church's influence on obstetric practice during one of my county relief sojourns in a small district hospital. There were no other junior medical staff, so I was doing a caesarean section and tubal ligation on my own, with only the scrub nurse for assistance. This was fine as she was very skilled and used to carrying out the two roles of scrub nurse and surgical assistant. The patient was a Protestant and the nurse was Catholic.

After delivering the baby and closing the opening in the uterus, I turned my attention to the tubal ligation. The nurse laid out the instruments and suture material I would need and said:

"I hope you don't mind, Doctor, I know the patient is Protestant, but I'm

Catholic, so I can't be part of the sterilisation operation. I think you have everything you need there to tie the tubes, and I'll be back to assist immediately you're finished."

With that, she left her side of the operating table, moved into the corner of the room, and turned her back to me. Tubal ligation is a very simple procedure and was easily done on my own with the instruments she had neatly laid out.

"Sorry about this. Do you have everything you need, Doctor?"

"Yes, thank you, Nurse, all's well here. I'll be done in a minute, then you can join me for the finale."

I had no problem with this. She was so efficient and helpful, that a short intermission on her part for personal reasons was acceptable to me.

I don't think any of us who tried to navigate and, when possible, defy the Church's repressive control of women's reproduction in Ireland, could have anticipated the events of May 2018. It was then, fifty years after Pope Paul's disastrous encyclical (disastrous for both the Church's authority and the diminishing number of women willing to follow the ruling), that the population of the Republic of Ireland decisively voted in the most extreme form of birth control – termination of pregnancy. In essence, they turned their voting gaze toward the Vatican and declared, 'Enough, we're not going to take it anymore.'

Good for them.

****

After six years I had acquired two postgraduate fellowship degrees and had a lot of clinical experience. It was time to look at gaining some overseas credentials. This was usually sought in North America; the so-called BTA (Been to America) degree.

There was another consideration – job prospects in Ireland and the UK were generally abysmal. In 1968, the Junior Hospital Doctors Association was formed with the aim of providing statistics on the availability of consultant posts in the various specialties in the UK. This confirmed, in stark numbers, just how broad-based the pyramid of junior doctors was and how few consultant positions there were in comparison.

The Association provided tables for each specialty with the numbers of junior doctors in each rank, along with the number and ages of the incumbent consultants. This showed the imbalance between the number of senior registrar and consultant positions, and the waiting period before each consultant vacancy. This was particularly long in the surgical specialties, including obstetrics and gynaecology. Whereas in some disciplines, such as anaesthesia and the medical subspecialties, there was opportunity for rapid advancement.

Historically, both the north and south of Ireland have always overproduced graduates in the professions: architects, doctors, engineers, lawyers, nurses and teachers. Looking at my medical graduate's year photograph, only one third of our class made their career in Northern Ireland. Of the rest, a handful settled elsewhere in the UK. The majority of our class, about sixty percent, had to move outside the UK for long-term employment. Most of these went to Australia, Canada, New Zealand, South Africa and the United States which, luckily for us, needed more doctors than they produced.

There seemed to be no long-term planning by those responsible for appointing new consultants. It was mostly a case of hanging on long enough until a post came up and, if it was your turn, you got it. To some extent, those with get up and go, got up and went. I think the powers that be were glad so many of us moved overseas to find work – it saved them from the embarrassment of too many well qualified people for too few jobs.

Accordingly, in July 1970, I took up an appointment as a senior resident in obstetrics and gynaecology at the Women's Pavilion of the Winnipeg General Hospital at the University of Manitoba. The department head was Doctor Mervyn Roulston, himself a former Queen's Belfast graduate.

In 1967, Canada established Medicare for all citizens – similar to the National Health Service in the UK. As a result, there was a huge increase in demand for medical practitioners and their services, which exceeded the output of Canadian medical schools. Doctors from the UK and Commonwealth countries were actively recruited to fill the need. By the late 1970s, about one quarter of all practicing doctors in Canada came from those countries. I was one of that cohort.

No matter how strong the stimulus, or how welcoming the reception, it's a hard decision to leave your homeland.

Chapter 26
Up North

I spent the 1970s in Winnipeg and during that time, as well as my job in obstetrics and gynaecology at the Winnipeg General Hospital (WGH), I worked with the Northern Medical Unit (NMU) of the University of Manitoba. The director of the unit, which started in 1970, was Doctor Jack Hildes – a man I came to admire. He was an internist who had carried out studies in the Canadian Arctic and had a deep feeling for and understanding of the north and the medical problems facing its people.

The unit was established to provide general practitioners and specialist consultant back up for the regional hospitals and small settlements of the indigenous people of northern Manitoba. In addition, from the hospital in Churchill on the northern edge of Manitoba, they served the nursing stations of the eight Inuit settlements in the Central Canadian Arctic. Churchill's medical services had formerly been provided by the Canadian military at the Fort Churchill General Hospital, up until their withdrawal from the Fort Churchill base in the late 1960s. Hildes put together a cadre of specialist consultants from Winnipeg whom he felt had the appropriate outlook for northern service.

During my year as a resident at the WGH I did encounter a few patients from these small communities in northern Manitoba and the Arctic. My first trip to Churchill was unplanned and precipitous; it came in August 1971, at the end of my year as a resident. On Sunday afternoon I was in hospital studying for my forthcoming Canadian specialty exams when a call came in for the consultant obstetrician on duty in the hospital - one Jean McFarlane. The call was from one of the GPs in Churchill about a woman in obstructed labour who they thought might need a caesarean section. They had no surgical or anaesthetic expertise available – could Jean arrange to send up an obstetrician? They were always aware of the flight schedules between Winnipeg and Churchill and knew there was one leaving in about an hour, hence the timing of the call.

Jean McFarlane and I were in the coffee room adjacent to the labour floor when she took the call.

"Right, Tom Baskett, how would you like to see the Canadian north and do a caesarean section at no cost or remuneration to yourself," she chuckled.

"I thought you'd never ask," I replied.

"Sold," she said. "I always knew the Irish were insane and thank goodness for that. Oh, and by the way, there's no anaesthetist, so you'll have to do it under local."

I phoned my wife who quickly came to the hospital and drove me to the airport. Fortuitously, Jack Hildes was already booked on this flight for one of his routine administrative trips to Churchill. So, we met for the first time on the Trans Air flight, which took about two-and-a-half hours for the 1500 kilometre journey.

During the flight Jack chatted to me about the north and the role of the Northern Medical Unit; in his own quiet understated manner his love of the area and its people shone through. Before leaving the hospital, I had taken an old obstetric text from the small library in the obstetrics and gynaecology department. I told Jack I had never done a caesarean under local anaesthesia before so, I took a bit of time to read up on it as we flew.

We were met at Churchill airport by one of the GPs who drove us straight to the labour ward of the hospital. The patient was an Inuit woman, Irene Tookoolook, from one of the small arctic communities north of Churchill. She was twenty-eight years old and had delivered three children in the past without complication. She spoke English, as most of those under forty years of age did; for those over forty we usually needed an interpreter.

The GP looking after her was Karen Shaw, a good doctor whom I knew from the previous year when she was an intern on our unit. She told Mrs. Tookoolook who I was and then backed away. Irene Tookoolook gave me a look of acknowledgment from her pain-etched face. She was sweating from her effort to push the baby out, but well in control of herself. This was something I would come to learn – just how well Inuit women seemed to cope with labour. I went over and took her hand.

"Hello, Mrs. Tookoolook, I'm Doctor Baskett that Doctor Shaw has told you about. I'm an obstetrician and I just need to examine you to see why your baby is being so stubborn."

"Yes, Doctor."

I did an internal examination and confirmed that the cervix was fully open and the baby's head had progressed well down the pelvic canal. However, I was able to feel the baby's eyebrows - which in a normally progressive labour one should not. Here was the cause of her obstructed labour, the baby's head had angled backwards as it came down the pelvic canal. This was called a brow presentation and was the largest diameter of the baby's head - too large for Irene Tookoolook to push out, no matter how heroic her efforts. The only solution was either delivery by caesarean section or to somehow angle and flex the baby's head forward – in essence push its chin toward its chest. This would produce the normal, smallest diameter and allow safe vaginal delivery.

"Can you get me a pair of Kielland's forceps?" I asked Karen.

"All the forceps are right here" she said, handling several bundles on the table beside her …."Yes, here are the Kiellands."

Kielland's forceps, introduced in 1915, were specifically designed to allow safe rotation of the baby's head. It wasn't often done for brow presentation, but if one could rotate the baby's head it sometimes helped change the angle and flex it to the desired smaller diameter. If it worked, great, if not it could make things worse and impede the oxygen supply to the baby. So, another of those buttock-clenching moments – not uncommon in obstetrics. I had done this manoeuvre twice before, but ideally it should be done under full anaesthesia, and we had no safe way of doing that. On balance, however, I thought it worth a try as the alternative, caesarean under local, was probably more risky - especially to Mrs. Tookoolook.

"Mrs. Tookoolook, the position of the baby's head in your pelvis is making it impossible for you to push it out. I can use these forceps to cradle the baby's head and change the position, so you can deliver yourself. I will put some freezing anaesthetic down below and Doctor Shaw will give you a mask to breathe with gas that will help. But you will still feel a lot of pressure."

Between her still herculean efforts she nodded agreement. The only safe gas to use was a nitrous oxide/oxygen mix which would only slightly dull her senses.

We put her legs up in supporting stirrups and I used a lot of local anaesthetic to block the two main pudendal nerves that supply the lower vagina and perineum. While Karen gave the gas mix, I gently applied the forceps blades along the side of the baby's head. With the handle of the forceps …. Slowly and gently…. No force …. Check the blades aren't slipping …. Right hand down a bit …. Turning? …. Flexing? …. OK. To my delight it went smoothly, and the baby's head flexed to the normal position. I removed the forceps blades, stopped the gas inhalation and with the next contraction she was able to push her baby out into my waiting hands.

Mrs. Tookoolook gave the most beautiful wide smile of relief and triumph – matched by my behind-my-mask grin of pride. 'Well done, Baskett,' I said to myself; it was one of those moments when you know you have accomplished something quite splendid, and that no one else in the room really has any idea what you have achieved, so quiet self-congratulation is allowed. Also, to acknowledge that a huge, 'Well done, Mrs. Tookoolook' took priority.

Throughout these proceedings Jack Hildes had been unobtrusively on the periphery, presumably seeing how I handled the situation. I must have met his standards, as on the return journey he asked if I would become an obstetrics and gynaecology consultant to the NMU. I said I would and did so for the next nine years. I always felt it was some of the best and most fulfilling work I have done. I developed a huge admiration for the people of the north whose ingenuity and tenacity in a tough environment were remarkable. Some of my encounters with northern medicine are outlined in other chapters.

Chapter 27
He's a Lovely Man

As consultants to the Northern Medical Unit we undertook visits to Churchill every two months or so. These were planned to reduce the need for patients from the north to travel out to Winnipeg for specialist consultation. Patients from the eight small Arctic communities would have to come to Churchill but would be spared the long Churchill to Winnipeg commute.

Usually, three or four of us would travel up together; anaesthetist, myself, and one or two other consultants, in such specialties as psychiatry and paediatrics. Over two or three days we would conduct clinics and I would also do minor gynaecological surgery. We would use the surgical sessions to teach two of the four Churchill general practitioners extra skills – one in anaesthesia and one in basic surgical technique. The idea was, with this extra training, these GPs could cope better with surgical and gynaecological emergencies that might arise when we were not there.

We stayed at the Fort Churchill permanent married quarters (PMQs), one of which was available for visiting consultants. It was known as the Hildes Hilton – after Jack Hildes, director of the NMU. Our PMQ had three bedrooms, each with two beds, bathroom, kitchen, and a sitting/dining area. It was close to the Fort Churchill General Hospital. Adjacent PMQs were occupied by the GPs.

The flight from Winnipeg usually arrived in Churchill in the late afternoon. Our routine was to go to the Hudson's Bay store for groceries and to the liquor outlet for beer and wine. Most of our culinary skills were minimal, so the meals were pretty basic.

One such trip in the early 1970s started routinely but led to a bit of a dent to my reputation. We had arrived, shopped, and settled in as usual. The evening menu was fried fish fingers and chips (French fries), accompanied by a glass of indifferent Italian red wine. I had started feeling unwell just before we landed but put it down to motion sickness. However, after supper I began to feel nauseated and regretted taking the meal and wine.

About eight o'clock in the evening the phone rang in the Hildes Hilton and I answered.

"Tom, thank goodness you're there," said Sharon Dooley, one of the local GPs that I knew well. "I've got one of the teachers here in labour, I'm pretty sure it's a breech and I've never delivered one before. She's almost fully dilated, can you come right away?" she said urgently.

"On my way."

Almost fully dilated meant that the cervix was nearly completely open and that delivery would soon follow. The fact that the breech was coming first added many potential risks to the baby during delivery. This was something that specialist obstetricians trained for and, in that era, expertise in delivery of a breech baby was considered by many to be the measure of an obstetrician. As junior obstetricians in training we spent many hours with medical mannequins of the pelvis and a fetal doll practising the manoeuvres for safe delivery of the breech baby. We used to recite all the manoeuvres and their timing as we did them. This learning by repetition and rote was a great help when faced with the real thing.

Sharon met me just outside the labour and delivery room, she was pretty wound up.

"She's one of our local teachers and this is her second baby. Her first delivery was normal. I thought this labour was going the same way, until late on when I found she was breech. She's really moving on. Her husband is with her."

"What are their names?" I asked.

"Ann and Joe Sprague. I've given you a bit of a build-up. Told them you are a very experienced obstetrician and an expert at delivering breeches and how lucky they are that you're here. Her mother was from Dublin, so I laid it on about you being a lovely Irish man – hope you don't mind."

"You omitted the part about my being able to walk on water," I said, and got a sharp punch on the arm for my trouble.

We went in and she introduced me.

"Hello Mrs. Sprague and hello Mister Sprague, extreme circumstances I know, but I'm pleased to meet you." In view of Sharon's build-up, I laid on the Irish accent and chat for the next minute or so. Not the full 'faith and begorra' version, just a mild touch of the Irish ethnics – northern variety.

No time to change into scrubs: I just rolled up my sleeves, got into a gown, quick scrub-up of my hands at the adjacent sink and put on sterile gloves. I was now being hit by regular waves of severe nausea.

Mrs. Sprague was doing very well and coping with her pains. I examined her, and the cervix was now fully dilated and the breech of the baby had descended well into the lower pelvis – so far, so good.

"Mrs. Sprague, as Doctor Dooley said, your baby is coming bottom-first, but he's descending well in a good position, so we'll be OK." With a bottom-first presentation it is obviously possible to tell the sex of the baby just before delivery.

"You can tell it's a boy, Doctor?" Mrs. Sprague said excitedly.

"Indeed, he is, and very obviously so," I said

"A baby brother for your daughter to boss around," said Sharon.

"Now, Mrs. Sprague, you can start pushing your baby out. I'm going to put some freezing down here as I will need to make a small cut to help him out. There will still be a lot of pressure during his delivery, because of his position. At a later point I will ask you to stop pushing, even though you will still want to – it's very important that you do exactly what I say."

"OK, Doctor."

I was still feeling nauseated, but the excitement and concentration was holding it off, as I quickly put in a local nerve block.

Mrs. Sprague was a real trooper and pushing well. I went into my well-rehearsed breech delivery routine:

Hands off, until the baby's bottom rises up over the perineum …. Episiotomy at the start of the next contraction …. Deliver the breech …. Assist delivery of the legs …. Keep the baby's back upwards …. Allow her to push the baby's chest out …. Deliver the arms by putting two fingers over each shoulder in turn and gently hooking them down …. Keep the baby's back upwards …. Stop pushing …. Place the baby's body astride my right forearm …. Put first and second fingers of right hand on either side of baby's nose and press down to flex his head …. With left hand's fingers push forward on the back of the baby's head to flex it …. Flexed is smallest diameter …. No pushing …. With both hands now controlling and flexing the head, gently deliver it up and out …. Yes …. Well done all.

Sharon clamped and cut the cord. I handed the baby boy off to her. He had that slightly stunned look that breech baby's have. After all, their head has come through the pelvis in two or three minutes, compared to the hours with the normal head-first delivery. He soon cried and made all the appropriate movements and noises.

Now the concentration and tension were over I was very nauseated and knew it was just a matter of time before I was sick. It was the delivery of the placenta that finished me. I was sitting on the small stool with wheels that allows you to move around as you do the delivery manoeuvres. From this position between the patient's legs, I propelled myself on the mobile stool across the floor to the scrub-up sink, leant over and threw up. This was not a quiet discreet vomit, but a full-on stomach-emptying job.

"Stomach flu," I mumbled.

The fish fingers and chips did not make for efficient drainage from the sink. The overwhelming aroma, however, wafting across the delivery room was that of cheap Italian Chianti wine. The Sprague's initial response of relief and joy at the safe delivery of their son (not to be called Thomas, I now suspected) was replaced by looks of disgust. The lovely Irish obstetrician had been transformed into a common Irish drunk – 'stomach flu', indeed.

I left Doctor Dooley to sew up the episiotomy.

You can't win them all. At least the mother and baby were unscathed.

Chapter 28
She's Still Bleeding

The phone rang at three a.m. on a Sunday morning in June 1972.
"Tom, its Jack Hildes – sorry to wake you but we've got a bit of an obstetric emergency up north."
"No problem," I lied. "What's up?"
"There's a woman on a reserve with no nurse who just delivered and she's still bleeding – pretty heavily it seems."

He mentioned the name of a small Indian reserve community northeast of Winnipeg on the edge of Lake Winnipeg. This was a 'fly-in' reserve with no roads. It was a single-nurse station. The nurse had gone on leave but there was no replacement, only an untrained local woman who worked as an assistant to the nurse. The patient in question was thirty-eight-year-old, Mrs. Sandy Bear, who had just delivered her tenth baby in the nursing station.

The only communication was indirect by radiophone and via this means I instructed the assistant to find the glass ampoule of ergometrine* in the medication cupboard, how to break the top off, put a needle and syringe together and where to inject it into Mrs. Bear's thigh. From the garbled communication it seemed that the bleeding had been very heavy but had since diminished. The placenta was not delivered and the umbilical cord had broken off when the assistant pulled on it to try and deliver the placenta. I told her to keep Mrs. Bear flat and put her legs up on pillows to reduce the shock. Also, to feel her tummy just above the pubic bone for the uterus, which should be the size of a softball, and to rub it to keep it hard. In addition to drugs, massage of the uterus could help it contract and stem the bleeding; a well-contracted uterus is firm and hard to the touch.

"Someone's going to have to go up and get her," said Jack.
"I suppose that would be me," I said.
"I knew you would see the light."
"It's three a.m. and I don't see any light."

---

*The commonest cause of bleeding after delivery is relaxation of the muscles of the uterus (womb); ergometrine is a life-saving drug that causes the musculature of the uterus to contract which closes the blood vessels and stops the bleeding.

"That's the other thing," Jack said. "There is an air-field, but it's a visual daylight-only landing strip."

Luckily it was June and it would soon be dawn. Jack had arranged the pilot and plane; a small, chartered, single-engine job. He picked me up at my home at about four a.m. and drove to the nearby Winnipeg airport. We didn't go through the normal entrance but drove around the perimeter to a hangar at the back of the airport. There was a light on and the pilot was pushing open the door.

"That's you," said Jack. "Let me know how it turns out. Good luck."

I went over and met the pilot, one Jake Melnyk. I helped him pull the small plane out of the hangar. It was a six-seater and we removed the four back seats in anticipation of the need to put the patient on a stretcher in the back.

"It's about sixty to seventy minutes flying time, so we'll leave just before five to get there with enough light to land," Jake said.

We took off and headed north-east, flying into one of those beautiful Manitoba dawns in a cloudless sky. Jake knew the area well and we flew over the small settlement, landing smoothly on the airstrip, a mix of gravel and weeds carved out in the adjacent woods.

"I'll stay with the plane," said Jake. "You'll find the trail to the houses over there by the big rock."

I walked about one hundred metres along a path through the trees and into the collection of small houses. I had expected to be met by a reception party and an enthusiastic welcome for the medical saviour. Instead, there was total silence and no one in sight. I walked on and saw the profile of the nursing station; outside was a man squatting on his haunches who looked quite uninterested in my presence.

"I'm the doctor, is the patient here?"

"Inside," he said.

I went into the nursing station and was met by the assistant, Clara Spence, an elderly woman with a kind worried face.

"Thanks for coming, Doctor, she's in here."

I found Mrs. Bear in the next room lying in a bed on top of a rumpled pile of sheets covered in blood and clots – she had clearly lost a lot of blood. Her baby daughter was wrapped up in an adjacent cot – fast asleep and oblivious to the trouble her delivery had caused her mother.

"Mrs. Bear, I'm, Doctor Baskett, an obstetrician from Winnipeg, I've come to help."

"Thank you, Doctor."

She was pale and clammy, with a rapid pulse and low blood pressure – the classic picture of shock from severe blood loss. She also had that frightened stunned look of someone undergoing a life-threatening experience. I checked, and she was not bleeding much now. Feeling her uterus in her lower abdomen, I was happy to find it hard and firmly contracted – the ergometrine had obviously done its work.

Mrs. Spence was clearly upset and worried.

"A few minutes after the baby came, she started to bleed …. It was a lot …. It was so much I could hear it* …. That's when I got on the radio for help."

I reassured her, "You did the right thing, and the injection you gave seems to have worked – so, well done."

"Mrs. Bear, I need to start an intravenous drip and put some salt solution into your veins because, as you know, you've lost a lot of blood."

I started the IV and ran in the saline solution at full speed. I got one litre into her and began another. I examined her vaginally and found the cervix closed around the placenta. There was only slight bleeding.

The proper treatment was to remove the placenta, but I would need an anaesthetic to do this. The only option was to minimise the bleeding by keeping the uterus contracted around the placenta. If this failed and she bled heavily again it could be catastrophic. I added another drug, oxytocin, to the saline solution which should keep the uterus contracted and stem the bleeding, but I needed to get her out to hospital.

"Mrs. Bear, the bleeding is under control, so we're OK. We're going to have to take you to hospital in Winnipeg and give you an anaesthetic so we can remove the afterbirth. You will also need a blood transfusion. Is your husband here?"

"That's him outside," said the assistant.

---

* Those who practice midwifery and obstetrics are familiar with the term 'audible' haemorrhage – bleeding so profuse you can hear it flow like a tap. It can also induce a 'buttock-clenching' reflex in the observer – another response familiar to those with serious clinical experience.

I went outside and explained the situation to Mr. Bear, and told him, "You need to get three of your friends to help carry your wife on a stretcher to the plane. I'm sorry there won't be room for anyone else, so, you'll have to come out on the next sked." *

There was a stretcher in the nursing station, so I cleaned Mrs. Bear up as much as possible and got her onto the stretcher with fresh blankets. As a medical student I had been a member of the Royal Army Medical Corps (RAMC) in the Officers Training Corps at Queen's University. (Equivalent to the Army Reserve in Canada.) One of the things I remembered was the precision required for stretcher bearers. Unless all four inside legs of the bearers move in unison the person on the stretcher is bounced along roughly. I explained this to my four stretcher bearers and started them off with: 'Inside leg, forward march .... One, two .... One, two etc.' With me holding up the IV bag of saline and calling the cadence we moved smoothly through the path in the woods to the plane. I was quietly but hugely proud of myself for remembering this piece of, now applicable, military medicine. Unfortunately, it didn't do anything to combat the effing mosquitoes.

We gently manoeuvred the stretcher into the plane behind the two pilot seats. Mr. Bear leaned in, and said a few words to his wife, kissed her cheek and left. I checked her over: minimal bleeding, nice firm uterus, reasonable pulse and blood pressure – we should be all right, as long as she didn't start bleeding again.

I hung the third litre bag of saline and oxytocin on the wall of the plane and put the infusion rate to a slower maintenance level. I had put a catheter in her bladder at the nursing station, as she would have no opportunity to pee. Neither would I for that matter, so I took a quick side trip into the woods before take-off.

I checked her periodically on the return flight.

"Are you doing all right back there Mrs. Bear?"

"Yes, I'm OK, Doctor."

I hung over the back of my seat, pretzel-shaped, to check her blood loss and confirm that her uterus was still hard.

"We're all right now, you're going to be OK."

"Thanks, Doctor."

*Sked=Scheduled flight: schedule was usually pronounced 'skedule' and known by the abbreviated word 'sked.'

We radioed ahead to the airport and arranged for an ambulance to meet us. Thence, to the Women's Pavilion—the maternity and gynaecology unit of the Winnipeg General Hospital. There we gave her a three-unit blood transfusion and I removed her placenta under anaesthesia.

She recovered but was weak and a bit 'shell-shocked.' We chatted a lot about what had happened and, not surprisingly, she was adamant that this would be her last pregnancy. As this was her tenth, it seemed like a reasonable, if overdue decision.

Two days later on my morning round I found Mr. Bear asleep on the floor under his wife's bed. It was pretty resourceful of him to get to Winnipeg and beat the system sufficiently to spend the night on the floor in his wife's hospital room. I took him out into the corridor, and we had a long talk about his wife's near-miss, and about birth control. To my surprise he accepted the option of vasectomy and, even more surprisingly, he later went through with it.

Mr. Bear was a man of few words, but he came through for his wife on this occasion. As he said, "She's done enough."

Good on you, Mr. Bear.

Chapter 29
Arctic Family Planning

In the early 1970s I got to know the nurse/midwives in the Arctic settlements and the GPs in Churchill. They also got to know me. At that time all midwives had full training as registered nurses before they undertook their midwifery education. Thus, as fully qualified and experienced nurse/midwives they, in a sense, acted as the GP for the settlement they served and lived in.

One such British-trained nurse/midwife (I'll call her Carol) in one of the settlements I was to visit decided it would be a good idea if I gave a talk to the local men on family planning and birth control. The stimulus for this was the fact that local Inuit women were having larger families than before. This was, at least in part, due to their adoption of bottle feeding for their infants as opposed to their previous use of breast feeding alone. Complete breast feeding imparts a natural period of protection from pregnancy, often up to three or four years. Bottle feeding on the other hand provided no such protection and pregnancies could and were becoming almost an annual event.

The women were receptive to the nurse's explanation of birth control methods but, for the commonest method (sterilisation by tubal ligation), the husband's consent was needed as well as that of the wife. (The same applied to male sterilisation. The wife had to give consent). The nurse felt the men were not receptive to a female (nurse) advocating and explaining tubal ligation as an option for their wives. Hence, she 'volunteered' me to fill this role. Before my visit, notices were put up around the community advertising the 'expert doctor' from Winnipeg who would explain all at a men-only meeting in the community hall at an appointed hour.

"I hope you don't mind," she explained, as I stepped off the afternoon flight from Churchill. ".... but I have sort of arranged for you to speak to the men of the settlement."

"Sort of?"

"Well, actually it's all arranged, for six o'clock this evening."

"What am I supposed to be talking about?"

"Birth control and family planning."

"Oh, whoopee …. but many of them won't understand English."

"That's OK, I've arranged for John, our nursing station janitor and handyman to accompany you and translate."

I knew John from my previous visit. As a young Inuit he would be fluent in both English and his native Inuktitut.

"I bet he's not keen,"

"Not in the least – but I've threatened him with unemployment if he refuses."

"In the best traditions of the gentle, caring, nursing profession, I suppose."

"Exactly – but I do promise you both a slap-up dinner after the meeting."

"Oh, that should make it all better, then."

"I knew you'd agree."

The community hall was a trailer (caravan), so John and I turned up there at the appointed hour. John was even less enthusiastic than I was. In the Inuit culture it was very difficult for the younger generation to discuss intimate medical matters with their elders. We had, to a degree, the same problem with young female translators when taking a medical history and giving advice to older Inuit women in the clinics.

The hall was empty of furniture except for two chairs placed at the front for John and me. The rest of the place was already full of adult men, ranging from their early twenties to extreme old age. They sat on the floor in a semi-circle in front of our chairs.

I was quite nervous and intimidated by the whole setup. On such occasions, I could become almost detached from the situation – as though I was looking down with a birds-eye view of the scene. (I sometimes had the same sensation when under stress at the start of an oral examination, during important medical school exams). The feeling lasted only a few seconds, during which I thought, if the lads from my medical class in Belfast could see me now there would be much knee-slapping laughter and ridicule at my expense.

I started the meeting with the usual introductory platitudes, as John manifested his discomfort by undertaking a detailed, head-down study of his boots – which he sustained for most of the meeting. I stopped after every two or three sentences to allow John to translate, which, despite his reluctance, he seemed to do well. From the start I emphasised that I hoped this would be a discussion rather than just a talk by me, and that I encouraged questions and comments from the audience at any time. None were forthcoming.

I ploughed on, outlining the various methods of contraception, and described the benefits for the woman's overall health of gaps between pregnancies longer than twelve to eighteen months. Further encouragement for audience participation continued to elicit no response. I finished by covering in detail the choice of sterilisation by tubal ligation for women and by vasectomy for men, for those who felt their family was complete. Still, no audience participation. So, I told John to tell them, that was all, I was finished.

I was about to leave when one very elderly man rose unsteadily to his feet – John translated. The elder thanked the doctor for coming and for the talk. He also said he had noticed that women in the community became very tired after they had a lot of children.

So, that was it. I returned to the nursing station feeling defeated and somewhat depressed. I apologised to nurse Carol, telling her I thought it had been a failure – citing the lack of audience involvement. I told her of the lone elder's brief comments. She said it was not a surprise that only he would speak on behalf of the whole group – it would be disrespectful for others to offer an opinion. In fact, she felt that far from being a failure, the elder's words were tantamount to an endorsement for birth control and family planning. So, as it turned out, mission accomplished.

John and I had the promised slap-up dinner - fried caribou steak and chips.

*

There is an interesting and universal observation about family planning and birth control. When the number of infant and childhood deaths fall to low levels, women became secure about the survival of their offspring and seek out and avail themselves of birth control methods. The other factor strongly related to the use of birth control is female literacy.

In the mid 1970s, an allegation was made by a representative of the Catholic church that Inuit women were being subjected to "intensive sterilisation." Partly in response to this accusation, we undertook a study of female sterilisation in our area of the Central Canadian Arctic, which included Churchill and the eight settlements served by the Northern Medical Unit. Comparing the Caucasian and Inuit residents at the time of tubal ligation, we found that Inuit women were on average three years older and had twice as many children (8.3 versus 4.0) as their Caucasian counterparts.

Chapter 30
Seventh Son

In the so-called modern developed world, with the near ubiquitous use of antenatal ultrasound, most parents know the sex of their infant before birth – which I think rather takes the fun out of it. During my career there were occasions when the odds defied the prediction of fetal sex. I once looked after a colleague's wife in three pregnancies and each time delivered her of a daughter by caesarean section. During her fourth pregnancy she and her family spent some time in the USA where a routine antenatal ultrasound led to her being told she was going to have another girl. She was quite annoyed as she did not want to know this before delivery, and was to a degree disappointed to have a fourth child of the same sex. They returned to Canada at the end of her pregnancy, and I arranged and later performed her fourth caesarean delivery. To all our surprise, and to the immense delight of the parents, it turned out that the ultrasound had been misinterpreted and the normal healthy infant I delivered was a boy. I don't think I have ever known a baby's arrival welcomed with greater joy. [However, they missed a potential financial windfall by not suing, in the best American tradition, for severe 'pain and suffering.']

In 1970's Winnipeg, before smoking became a near-criminal offence, it was tradition that the father gave his friends and the obstetrician a cigar to celebrate the birth. It was a time before fathers routinely attended the actual delivery. There was a small room, often smoke-filled, at the end of the labour ward where expectant fathers waited. Immediately after delivery the obstetrician came to the room and told the father that his wife and newborn infant were fine – along with the infant's sex, birthweight, and other statistics - such as the impressive sound of the lusty bawls, hair colour, resemblance to famous people etc. (Although, in truth, many babies are not particularly attractive and start life with a face looking a bit like a squashed grapefruit – reflecting their sometimes-difficult passage into the world).

At this point the happy new father often produced a cigar as he proffered his thanks. One shrewd tobacco company had individual cigars wrapped in cellophane with, "It's a Girl," or, "It's a Boy" written on them. This ensured that the well-prepared father-to-be had to buy cigars with both designations, thereby doubling sales.

By the late 1970s it became *de rigueur* for fathers to attend the birth. Not all of them were keen and some felt under pressure to conform to this supportive role. In the early phase of labour the mother was in a room with a nurse and, usually, the father-to-be. When the birth was imminent, the mother was transferred across the hall to a more surgical delivery room. After transfer, the husband was bedecked in a surgical gown, cap and mask and taken along to join his wife. On one occasion things moved quickly and we forgot the husband. After the birth I went to the aforementioned smoke-filled waiting room to tell him the happy outcome and to apologise for not bringing him to the delivery. Before I could give my apology, he thanked me profusely for not making him attend the delivery, which he had been dreading. In fact, he was almost embarrassingly grateful. His wife later said, "Thank goodness, I knew he felt pressure to be with me, but he would have been useless, terrified and in the way. I was much better off with the nurse." About two weeks later six bottles of champagne were delivered to my house along with a heartfelt letter of thanks for helping him miss the delivery – no mention of how his newborn son was doing.

Early in my career in Winnipeg I looked after a woman – I'll call her Mrs. Sinclair. Her obstetric history was peculiar only for the fact that she had six previous pregnancies resulting in six sons. She was a healthy woman and all her pregnancies and deliveries had been uneventful. At that time there was no antenatal ultrasound diagnosis of fetal sex – so each birth offered up the 50:50 chance of either boy or girl. During her seventh labour there was much good-natured banter between the nurses and Mrs. Sinclair about the hoped-for daughter. The delivery was normal, and I received the infant who, of course, was a healthy baby boy. After clamping and dividing the umbilical cord, I held him up close to Mrs. Sinclair so she could see him in all his male glory. She looked him in the eye and said, with considerable feeling, "Awhh.... shit" – soon followed by more appropriate maternal noises as she cradled him in her arms.

At that time there was much talk about the importance of the first moments of mother-baby interaction as a vital component of maternal-infant bonding which was considered a very big deal. I wondered what the psychologists would have to say about the impact on a child's future mental stability when the first words his mum said to him were, "Awhh.... shit."

No impact at all I'm quite sure. Although I wouldn't put it past a canny lawyer to use this faecal reference as a defence in the event of any future law-breaking misdemeanours by said seventh son. On balance I think he was lucky to escape without some well-intentioned neonatal counselling.

The number seven has biblical, mystical, and superstitious significance. The seventh consecutive son (or daughter for that matter) was said to have special powers – particularly in the healing realm. Their touch could cure the King's evil (tuberculosis), and they were often sought out to, "chase away diseases and pains" by stroking the affected part. The chances of having seven sons in a row are 1 in 128, and with the modern small family size it has become a great rarity. The healing powers were even greater if you were the seventh son of a seventh son – a 1 in 16,000 long-shot. The ultimate was to be the seventh son of a seventh son born on the seventh day of the seventh month – try and top that lot!

As far as I know Mrs. Sinclair did not try for an eighth pregnancy when the odds of having a son or a daughter would still be 50:50. The chances of having eight consecutive sons are 1 in 256 – but she had already approached those odds by having seven in a row.

You have to know when to fold the cards you have been dealt.

Chapter 31

Polar Bear Alert

Churchill, Manitoba calls itself the Polar Bear Capital of the World, and with good reason. It lies in the southwest corner of Hudson's Bay, where several hundred polar bears spend the summer and early autumn. The bears live and hunt on sea-ice, which around Churchill melts in late July and does not reform until early November. Hence, the bears spend three months or so on the coast around the port of Churchill – close to which is one of the biggest polar bear denning areas in the world.

In the 1970s, and even more so to-day, polar bears were regarded as one of nature's treasures to be studied and protected. To this end, provincial government conservation officers actively surveyed the bears during September to November, when they were most active along the coast. In selected cases they would shoot a bear with a dart-syringe containing a strong sedative drug. This allowed them to study the bear, take blood samples and perhaps attach a location device to monitor their territorial movements. After removing the dart-syringe they left the animal, by now fairly disgruntled one imagines, to recover and continue its daily ambulation.

On one of my October trips to Churchill the hospital received an urgent call from one of the conservation officers – they had studied their comatose bear, but could not find the dart-syringe. Their credible worry was that the syringe had penetrated beneath the skin and could cause serious infection if not removed. They were pretty sure the dart had hit the front part of the bear. Was it feasible to x-ray this area of the animal? Was there a surgeon who might help find and remove the syringe?

Without my knowledge (I was doing a clinic), I was chosen by my fellow physicians as the closest thing to a surgeon. They told the conservation officer I would be happy to help and, no, I would not need any other doctors to assist me. They then informed me of this unique opportunity to add polar bear surgery to my rather thin academic curriculum vitae. The other 'volunteer' was the x-ray technician, who was instructed to get the portable x-ray machine down to the rear basement door of the hospital. To outside this door, the conservation crew, using a truck, had dragged the polar bear on a large wooden platform.

A short review here of some of the anatomical qualities of the polar bear is in order. Fully grown, as this one was, they can weigh more than 1000 pounds (500kg), they have huge webbed paws that have been known to decapitate other large mammals, such as humans, with one swipe. Their jaws and dentition are impressive. (Ironically, although of no immediate relevance, but of obstetrical interest to me, the polar bear pup only weighs about one pound (500g) at birth).

As I surveyed the large creature, I asked the conservation officer some skill-testing questions, which seemed relevant to my short-term wellbeing.

"How long do these drugs usually last?"

"It's variable."

"Are there any early warning signs before the bear regains consciousness and starts moving?"

"Again, variable – sometimes it can be quite sudden."

For obvious reasons, I found none of this reassuring.

However, I felt I should make an effort. I knelt beside the front of the bear, which was lying on its right side – they had shot it from its left side. The left eyelid was open, and the eye seemed to be sizing me up, but at least it wasn't moving (the eye that is). With my hands I started to fussle about in the chest fur of the bear – no dart-syringe there. I moved to the left shoulder, crouching in readiness for an Olympic-style sprinting exit, should the bear even so much as twitch. I felt around in the axilla of the bear's left forepaw and, lo and behold, I could feel the dart in a fold of skin. One could see how easily it could have been missed. It was easy to remove. No need for the x-ray, which probably would have been technically impossible anyway. I quickly reversed away from the bear and into the basement doorway. "Well done, Baskett," I said to myself, "piece of cake" – potential 'brown trouser' moment averted.

I returned to the clinic – no change of clothing required.

Chapter 32
The Sign of the Bloody Feet

With my regular visits to Churchill, I came to know the GPs, many of whom had done their training in Winnipeg. During 1972, I visited and did clinics at all of the eight Inuit settlements around the edge of Hudson's Bay served by the Northern Medical Unit. As a result, I became familiar with the local conditions, in particular the vagaries of travel and patient transfer in these fly-in communities of the remote Canadian Arctic. Each settlement had a nursing station staffed by one to three nurse/midwives – most of whom were from Britain or Australia. At that time there was no opportunity for Canadian nurses to get midwifery training in Canada. The population of the settlements ranged from 200 to 1000. Most of the nursing stations were made up of three trailers attached together in an H configuration. One of which was the clinic and one was the nurse's living quarters; these two were connected by a third storage trailer. It was in the storage area where I usually slept when visiting – you brought your own sleeping bag. Because of my regular visits the northern nurses and doctors often called me for any urgent or emergency consultations in obstetrics.

One winter morning I got a call from Sharon Dooley, one of the GPs in Churchill. In the early hours of that same morning, an Inuit woman in her first pregnancy had started bleeding. The patient, Amy Pitsolak, was thirty-four weeks pregnant and had woken to find herself bleeding heavily. She got up, dressed, and went immediately to the nursing station. Over the next hour the bleeding settled, she had no pain, and the baby's heart beat was normal. Fortuitously, there was a scheduled flight leaving the settlement for Churchill that morning, so the nurse put Mrs. Pitsolak on board.

By the time Dr. Dooley received the patient in the Churchill hospital the bleeding had started again. Sharon put up an intravenous drip with saline and phoned me.

"Tom, I've got a thirty-four weeker with an antepartum bleed."

"Tell me more."

"She's twenty-one and it's her first pregnancy. Antenatal care by the midwife in the nursing station had been normal, up until she bled this morning. The bleeding settled in transit, but it's started again – although it's fairly light at present. Her pulse is 96, her blood pressure is normal, but the lower part of her uterus is a bit painful and tender. I'm worried she may have the beginnings of an abruption. (Partial separation of the placenta from the wall of the uterus and dangerous for both the mother and her baby) I think she may have had quite a heavy bleed at the start."

"Does she have the sign of the bloody feet?"

"What the hell are you talking about, Tom?"

"It's an old-fashioned clinical sign that can give some idea of how much blood she has lost. If a patient gets up from her bed bleeding, and there is enough blood to run down her legs to reach both feet and soak the webs in between her toes—It's called the sign of the bloody feet, and is said to mean a blood loss of at least two pints. It may be a load of old cobblers, but it could give us a rough guide."

"Let me check."

I stayed on the phone while Sharon Dooley went to check Mrs. Pitsolak's feet. Sharon was back within a minute.

"You're right …. You bugger …. Where do you get these pre-historic medical gems?"

"All part of the rich tapestry of highly classified, specialist knowledge."

Despite her whimsical banter I could tell that Sharon was worried. I knew her well; she was an astute doctor with good antennae for potential trouble.

The daily scheduled flight from Churchill to Winnipeg had already left, so we had to decide whether Amy Pitsolak needed to come out on a charter plane, or could she wait until tomorrow's regular flight. Either way, she needed to come down to Winnipeg. She wasn't in labour, but with placental abruption she might start at any time and the baby would be premature; Churchill had no special neonatal care facility. After discussion, we decided that Sharon would check on the availability of a charter plane and see whether Mrs. Pitsolak's bleeding and pain would subside.

She called back an hour later; Amy Pitsolak had declared her clinical hand with further bleeding and increasing pain in the lower part of her uterus. Her pulse had risen to 104, although her BP was still normal at 120 over 75. Patients can lose 25-30% of their blood volume without major changes in their pulse and BP. Further bleeding however, particularly if sustained, can lead to rapid deterioration and severe, even catastrophic, shock. The blood bank in Churchill was ambulatory; that is, it depended on a roster of screened volunteers who would come to the hospital and donate blood if someone with their blood group needed it. Obviously, this would take some time.

Sharon Dooley had ascertained that there was a plane available. It was a DC-3, from one of those one-plane, one-pilot charter companies. The DC-3 was a former passenger aircraft from the 1940s, and a reliable work-horse plane that now served in remote areas of the Canadian north. It would take about three hours to reach Winnipeg. On balance, we both felt this was the best option. The GPs were short-staffed in Churchill, so Dr. Dooley could not accompany the patient. She assigned one of her most experienced nurses, Karen Sheridan, to make the trip with Mrs. Pitsolak. I knew Karen – the patient was in good hands. Shortly after the plane left Churchill Sharon phoned with her final update.

"I'm worried about her, Tom, I think she's deteriorating. I've asked the nurse to send reports via the pilot to the Winnipeg airport. Can you get in touch with them? You probably need to meet the plane with some blood. I hope the hell she's alright."

"I will. I think it was the best decision to get her out. I'll keep you posted."

I phoned the airport in Winnipeg, asked to speak to the manager and explained the position. I would need to meet the plane on the tarmac, could they phone me with any update that came from the nurse on the flight? Those were the days when you could do that sort of thing and everyone cooperated. Imagine making that request nowadays: it would probably just be a few minutes before you were greeted by the anti-terrorist armed response team.

It is impossible to hear adequately in a noisy plane to take an accurate blood pressure; relying, as it does, on listening with a stethoscope for the muffled sound in the artery of the patient's arm, as the blood pressure cuff is deflated. I remember having the same problem in the ambulance from my days with the obstetric flying squad in Belfast. You can get an approximate reading of the upper level only, by feeling for the patient's pulse as the cuff is deflated.

About half-way into the flight, I got a message from the nurse via the airport, "Tell Dr. Baskett he definitely needs to meet the plane and bring some blood. Amy's pulse is up and she's shocky. Tell him its touch and go."

I packed a bag with some essentials, took two units of O negative blood from the labour ward fridge in the Women's Pavilion, and drove to the airport. There I was met by a policeman; I cannot now remember why, but I was to go out onto the tarmac in a police car rather than an ambulance. The DC-3 would taxi to the side of the terminal and unload on the tarmac. We drove out to the area where the plane would come in.

Each unit of blood came in a small plastic bag and contained about 400 millilitres of the universal donor group of O negative blood. It needed to be warmed up before it could be safely transfused, but I didn't have the means to do that. In my haste, I hadn't thought of this – dumb move, Baskett. The police car heater was on – it was February and about twenty-five to thirty degrees below zero outside. We had about thirty minutes before the plane would arrive, but the heat in the car wouldn't warm the blood in that time. Sudden bright idea – I undid my coat and put one blood bag under each of my armpits, with only my shirt between the bag and my skin.

"Crank up the car heater to full blast please, Officer," I said, as I began to shiver. I spent the remaining waiting time like this as the blood warmed up to my body temperature – the perfect level for transfusion. Good recovery from your initial dumb move, Baskett – acting as an all-natural, organic and environmentally-friendly blood warming unit.

The DC-3 taxied in and the policeman drove right up to it. The entry door was behind the wing to the back of the aircraft, it opened outwards and two men, who had hitched a ride on the charter, helped me inside. Amy Pitsolak was lying across two seats on the left side. I remember being surprised at how steep the aisle forward between the seats seemed.

The nurse was hovering. "Did you bring the blood?"

"Got it here," I said, producing it, magician-like, from beneath my arms.

"Mrs.Pitsolak, I'm an obstetrician here to help. We're going to give you some blood and get you to hospital." She was definitely in severe shock from the blood loss. I put up one of the units of blood onto the existing IV and squeezed the bag to empty it into her veins at maximum speed.

As I started the second bag I asked: "Karen, what's her pulse and BP now?"

"Pulse 120, blood pressure eighty over nothing."

Still severe shock figures. The ambulance arrived and we transferred Mrs.

Pitsolak to it on a flexible canvas stretcher. I accompanied her and squeezed in the second unit of blood as we made our way to my hospital's labour ward.

Sadly, this story did not have a happy ending. As is often the case with placental abruption our patient came into a rapidly progressive labour. Her cervix was more than half dilated when we reached the hospital. We could not hear the baby's heartbeat – and our worst fears were confirmed shortly thereafter, when she delivered a stillborn baby boy. This was followed by a large amount of blood clots, confirming the placental abruption. The blood clots landed in my lap, soaking through my scrubs and into my underwear.

Amy Pitsolak needed another four units of blood transfusion and, under the circumstances, we were fortunate she survived – albeit with great sadness at the loss of her son.

The happiness-index was better in the long term; over the next four years she had two healthy children, born normally after uncomplicated pregnancies.

So, two bloody signs: bloody feet in the patient and bloody underpants in the obstetrician.

Chapter 33
Surgery by Phone

The General Practitioners (GPs) of the Northern Medical Unit in Churchill were almost all early on in their careers – one to two years after medical graduation. Most stayed in post for two or more years, during which they became very experienced in northern medicine. They did not, however, have the training or resources to carry out major surgery.

As outlined in chapter twenty-seven, during specialist visits to Churchill by general surgeons and by obstetrician/gynaecologists (O&G), we did minor surgical procedures. In my case this included cases of abdominal tubal ligation, which involved surgically opening the abdomen (laparotomy) to gain access to the fallopian tubes. During these operations we taught one of the local GPs how to open the abdomen and to become familiar with the surgical anatomy of the female pelvis. Similar training in anaesthesia was given by the anaesthetist to another of the GPs. In this way we sought to provide the GPs with relevant experience, in case they were faced with an emergency that needed surgical treatment via laparotomy.

In fact, such cases were rare. Most urgent surgical cases could be managed with medical treatment, pending the three-hour air transport to Winnipeg*. The main exception in obstetrics, when surgery involving laparotomy might be necessary in Churchill, was ectopic pregnancy. And so, it proved to be one Saturday afternoon in the early 1970s.

An ectopic pregnancy is one that occurs outside the normal uterine cavity. This happens in about one in a hundred pregnancies, most often in one of the two fallopian tubes – a tubal pregnancy. The sensitive pregnancy tests and ultrasound needed to make an early diagnosis of ectopic pregnancy were not available in Churchill in the 1970s. Hence, the diagnosis was made on the clinical signs and symptoms, which in the early stages of an ectopic could be unreliable. By the time a tubal pregnancy could be definitively diagnosed, the pregnancy might have broken through or ruptured the wall of the fallopian tube. Sometimes this rupture involved

For example: Over five years (1971-1975), 556 Inuit women delivered their babies in the settlements (218), or in Churchill (338), without the need for surgical delivery by caesarean section. An additional fifty-four women were transferred to Winnipeg for high-risk pregnancy complications, and ten of these were delivered by caesarean section.

a blood vessel leading to haemorrhage into the pelvic and abdominal cavities. This produced a dramatic and unmistakable clinical picture. If progressive, this haemorrhage could be fatal, so this was not a surgical emergency that could wait three hours for air transfer to Winnipeg.

The phone call came to me in Winnipeg from Bill Harrison, one of the GPs in Churchill that I knew well.

"I think I've got one of those ectopic pregnancies that cannot wait," he said briskly, without any introductory pleasantries.

"So, you've asked the question, 'Is she opening sick or watching sick,' and decided it's the first."

"Exactly, she's definitely opening sick."

This was an old and established surgical maxim in the clinical assessment of acute abdominal pain. It goes to the core of the critical decision – is the patient's condition serious enough to warrant immediate surgery, in the form of laparotomy, or can it be dealt with by non-surgical management and careful observation?

The young patient was from the Churchill area, and about eight weeks pregnant – but not in the uterus where it should be. Without going into the medical details, Harrison made a solid case for surgery in this case. The clinical signs and symptoms of a ruptured tubal pregnancy, with associated developing shock from blood loss were obvious. In fact, he had already mobilised the operating room (OR) team and arranged for donors to give blood. He was phoning from the OR.

"Who's going to give the anaesthetic?" I asked.

"Ted Corbett, he's done quite a few. He went to Winnipeg recently to have a concentrated month of anaesthesia experience – so we should be OK."

"Good. Make sure you tell him to set up two IV lines and to pour in the saline and the blood, when it comes. He should know that he may not catch up with the blood loss until you've opened her and stopped the bleeding."

Bill was a competent and confident doctor, and probably headed for a surgical training residency when he finished his time in Churchill. But he was sensible enough to know that he was in uncharted waters when it came to doing a laparotomy and dealing with a ruptured tubal pregnancy.

"I know I've done quite a few abdominal tubal ligations with you, but would you stay on the phone until I get things under control?"

"Of course. Do a lower midline incision, not the transverse bikini one we do for tubal ligation. The midline is quicker and easier to do – and it will save you about two or three minutes getting into her abdomen."

Before I could give him any more advice, he said, "I have to go and scrub now. The patient has just been wheeled into the OR. I'll get one of the nurses to cover the phone with you. Thanks." There was urgency in his voice.

The two OR nurses, Jill and Laura, were experienced and very competent – just the sort you need when you are up against it. Jill got on the phone with me, and Laura scrubbed in for the surgery.

Jill filled me in as they started.

"They've got two IVs running with saline and the first unit of blood has just been started. She is shocky, pulse 100 and blood pressure, ninety over sixty." Shock, but not catastrophic yet.

"Tell Bill, that once he opens the abdomen, blood may well up out of the incision and he won't be able to see anything. Get the assistant to use the suction tubing immediately, to draw away the blood."

Jill relayed events to me as they happened. the general anaesthetic went well – thank goodness for Ted's month with the anaesthetists in Winnipeg. Bill made the incision and as advertised, lots of blood was all they could see.

"Jill," I said, "I'm going to talk to you as though I am talking directly to Bill - so, please just relay what I say to him."

"Just put your hand in and find the uterus, it should be sitting up in the pool of blood in the lower pelvis."

"Grasp it and pull it up into the incision."

"With your other hand check on each side of the uterus for the swollen tube with the pregnancy in it. It will probably have a lot of blood clot attached to it."

"Tell, Laura to have two sponge forceps ready."

"Bill says the swollen tube is on the right," said Jill.

"OK, place one sponge forceps on each side of the tubal pregnancy. You can put the forceps on firmly and as deep as you can feel. Even though you can't see them, if you do happen to grasp bowel, the sponge forceps won't damage it."

"If you've got them placed properly the blood supply to each side of the tube should now be blocked by the sponge forceps,"

"So, the source of the bleeding should be controlled. If so, the suction should clear the blood, and you might even begin to see what you're doing."

Happily, that was the case. Ted could now catch up and cover the blood loss by transfusion. Bill could actually see what he was doing. Removing the tube with its pregnancy was straightforward and Bill was more than up to this surgical task.

By the time the abdominal incision was closed, the patient was stable, and everything was under control.

"Well done, everyone. Over and out from me. I shall toast you all with a large gin and tonic this evening."

Chapter 34
Sleep Well, Samantha

Near the end of my first year in Canada I was doing a three-month rotation in gynaecology at the Women's Pavilion, the obstetrics and gynaecology unit of the Winnipeg General Hospital. With holidays and illness, we were short-staffed, so as a resident I was doing alternate nights on call. In contrast to obstetric call, however, I could cover gynaecology from home.

It was then I encountered the worst case of cancer I have ever seen. The details are not necessary or appropriate here, but it was horrible for the patient and very distressing for those looking after her. She had been admitted a month earlier from rural Manitoba to the care of the on-duty senior consultant/staffman. The patient's name was Samantha, but she was known to most simply as Sam. Her cancer was beyond surgical removal and all other treatments: radiotherapy, chemotherapy and immunotherapy had failed to halt the progress of this most aggressive disease. In essence, she was in hospital for terminal comfort care.

Samantha was only twenty-seven years old, three years younger than me. Because I was on the ward every day and alternate nights, I got to know her and took on the challenge of trying to keep her comfortable. The consultant nominally in charge of her was upset that he could provide no effective treatment. It wasn't that he didn't care, he was a kind man, but in his frustration, he was withdrawing from involvement with Samantha. He approached me and said: "Tom, I don't have anything to offer her. You seem to get on well with her and you're close in age. Would you mind organising all her care and only involve me if you have to."

"Of course," I agreed.

We would chat each day and I took to spending some time with her on the evenings I was in and on call. She had no relatives and no visitors.

"Do you prefer to be called Samantha or Sam?" I asked.

"Most people just call me Sam, and that's OK, but I also like my full name."

"I'll call you Samantha, then."

"And I'll call you, Doctor Tom, if that's OK?"

"Of course, it is."

Samantha was of slender build with thick straight black hair and big, dark brown eyes. Even her slender build was rapidly wasting away as the malignancy took control of her body. She told me that she was adopted and did not know her biological or adoptive parents. From her earliest memory she had been in a succession of foster homes in small-town Manitoba. There was only one stable home she remembered with happiness. It was an older couple and she cherished, in particular, the kindness of the man. He was a farmer, and under his guidance she had learned to look after and love animals. She was most at ease when she spoke of these happy formative years of her life. She was sixteen when he died, and she was moved on to another home. Apart from this one happy period, her life had been one of abuse and abandonment.

I had also grown up on a farm and, to pass the time and distract her from worsening symptoms, I told her stories of my own: being chased by a bull, driving a tractor as a twelve-year old, waking up to see new lambs born during the night in the field beside our house, helping a blacksmith shoe a horse, being taught by a milk-maid how to milk a cow by hand.

Thus, despite our very different backgrounds we found surprising common ground and became comfortable with each other. She had no strong religious beliefs: "I see God only in animals, not in us," she said.

It became harder to control the bad effects of her disease. She needed a permanent catheter in her bladder because of cancer blocking the outlet. Over three particularly bad weeks she wasted away to almost no muscle and could no longer stand, even with assistance. She was plagued by persistent nausea and pain. I did the best I could with intravenous nutrition, anti-nausea and pain-relieving drugs, but it was becoming a losing battle and Samantha was near the end of her tether.

Fortunately for both of us the night nurse, Nancy Stewart, was one of those hugely competent and kind people. She was in her early fifties and had raised three children after her husband died young; doing night duty suited her home commitments. At a time when nurses in Canada were beginning to disregard the nursing uniform code, Nancy Stewart maintained the full all-white uniform, including the, by now rare, starched white cap with navy blue trim. She had a kind handsome face and carried an air of competence and compassion. Nurse Stewart was able to sustain Samantha through some increasingly bad nights.

But Samantha only had bad times now. I had a continuous intravenous with low-dose morphine going, but her pain broke through. When we talked, there were no more happy reminiscences, just questions about how much longer she had to put up with the pain and nausea.

Nancy Stewart phoned me in the evening at about nine o'clock. "I don't think she can take much more," she said. "None of it's working."

"I'll be right in." I drove in to the hospital.

"It's pretty bad is it, Samantha?"

"I can't do it anymore, Doctor Tom."

"I'll be back in a wee minute with some relief for you." I went to talk it over with nurse Nancy. "I'm going to give her full doses of morphine as intravenous shots until she's free of pain – what do you think?"

"I think it's time," she agreed.

The adult dose of fifteen milligrams of morphine could be given every three hours. If I gave it as a one-shot IV dose, on top of the background low dose she was already getting, it should give her respite. At this stage Samantha weighed less than seventy pounds.

I returned with the syringe. "This injection will give you relief and rest – sleep well Samantha, bless your heart," I said, as I emptied the syringe into her IV line.

"OK, Doctor Tom, thank you."

I sat with her and held her hand for the few minutes before she fell asleep. I stayed on the ward and periodically checked in on her – she was sleeping, and her breathing was slow and shallow. Three hours later I gave her another full IV dose of morphine; 'Patient still showing signs of pain and distress,' I wrote in her medical chart. Thirty minutes later she stopped breathing.

Nancy and I tidied things up – we didn't say much. I filled out the death certificate. As I left the ward Nancy said, "You did the right thing, Doctor Tom." That nearly finished me, but I held it together until I got into my car in the small parking lot behind the Women's Pavilion.

Getting close to and fond of terminally ill patients has its costs. "Thoughts that do often lie too deep for tears," as William Wordsworth put it. I sat in my car for half an hour before I could drive home.

Chapter 35
The Ethics of Life

I finished my resident training in 1971 and was appointed staff man (consultant) in obstetrics and gynaecology at the Winnipeg General Hospital. I now had an office which was next to that of the head of obstetrics; a very experienced, impressive and highly respected man - known as the 'chief'.

One morning, free of clinical duties, I was sitting in my office doing not very much when I received a phone call that sharpened up my early morning metabolism. The call was to the chief, but he was out of his office, so it was directed to me by his secretary. It came from a senior obstetrician in a community hospital about ninety kilometres from Winnipeg.

"I'm transferring a young woman to your hospital because she needs intensive care. Your chief should be involved."

"I'll see that he is. Just give me the details."

"She's a twenty-three-year-old with a normal first pregnancy. But her labour was long and about three hours ago I did a fairly difficult forceps delivery under general anaesthesia. The baby is fine, but there were some vaginal lacerations in the mother. I sutured them but she continued to bleed and I had to pack her vagina with a lot of gauze. Then she started to ooze blood through the packs. She needs a blood transfusion, but the family have religious objections and refuse any blood products. She is going to be admitted directly to your intensive care unit (ICU). There's nothing more I can do here - the family are adamant about no transfusion. They agree with her transfer to Winnipeg; maybe you can get them to see sense. Her name is Jane Evans and the ambulance has just left. The husband and others are following in a car."

"Right, I'll contact the chief and we will see her in the ICU immediately she arrives. I'll keep you posted."

"Thanks. Sorry about this but I'm really stuck. I'm worried she might not make it."

I tracked down the chief.

"You go and see her, Tom. Let me know if you need me. I'll be in my office."

Mrs. Evans had just been admitted when I got over to the ICU. She was in severe shock from the blood loss; with pale cold peripheries, fast pulse and low blood pressure. Moist strands of her mousy blond hair were plastered across her forehead. Blood was seeping around the pack at the entrance to her vagina. She was barely conscious. Her husband and three male elders of their church were hovering; "No blood," one of them said, staring at me.

I called the chief. "Sir, no time for details. She is in dire straits and I need you here now. If we don't transfuse her, she will die, and I need the heavy artillery to deal with the elders."

"I'm on my way."

I went back to Mrs. Evans. She was on her fifth litre of intravenous saline solution, but this would not sustain her for long in the face of continued blood loss.

"Mrs. Evans, you are in the intensive care unit of the Winnipeg General Hospital. I'm Dr. Baskett, an obstetrician. Your baby is fine, but you have lost a lot of blood. We have to stop the bleeding and you will need another anaesthetic to do that, but it won't be safe unless we give you a blood transfusion. We have everything here to make you better. You will be OK, but we have to give you a blood transfusion. I know you don't want that but we cannot avoid it."

She was looking at me but with minimal comprehension – she was fading away. Informed consent was impossible. You don't often see someone bleed to death in front of you, but she was on the slippery slope.

Her husband was at her bedside as I spoke. He was a small man slightly younger than me. His face was pale and thin, pinched with fatigue and strain. The poor man had endured a prolonged labour with his wife, feeling useless and unable to help as events descended into forceps delivery, uncontrolled bleeding and a trip to the ICU in another hospital. So, he was sleep deprived and now facing the possible death of his wife. I don't know if the elders included his father or his father-in-law, but they had been moved away from the bedside by the nurse.

I spoke softly, so that only he could hear me:

"Mr. Evans, we can probably control things and save your wife, but only if we give her blood – there really is no alternative I'm afraid. We can't wait any longer or it will be too late." He seemed too stunned to speak, but at least he did not offer any protest against transfusion.

To my great relief the chief arrived. He took a couple of minutes with me and the senior physician of the ICU to size up the situation. Then he went straight over to the husband, put his arm around his shoulders and guided him over to face the group of elders.

"This young mother will not die in our hospital. We can save her but only with blood transfusion, so we will transfuse her. If you are opposed you will have to take her elsewhere."

This, of course, put them in an impossible situation. After a glaring standoff lasting about thirty seconds, they retired muttering. We started the blood.

The husband by now was completely overwhelmed. He sank to his knees sobbing and gasping, tears were streaming down his face and mucus was flowing from his nose and mouth – he was a complete wreck. The ICU nurse was quickly to his side. She put her arm around him and with a handful of tissues gently cleaned his face.

"It's OK, Mr. Evans, everything will be alright now, It's OK, It's OK. We have everything here. It will be OK."

Thank goodness for nurses; perfect timing with a handful of tissues and the sympathetic recognition that he too was suffering. As one of my physician friends once said to me, "When I grow up, I want to be a nurse." The chief too, had in a sense allied himself with Mr. Evans by putting an arm across his shoulders as he confronted the elders.

Now we could get on with catching up on the blood loss. Her admission blood test showed her haemoglobin (the essential oxygen-carrying red blood cells) to be five – less than half it should be. The full power of the ICU staff was unleashed and we poured in blood via two intravenous lines. I still had to find and stop the source of her bleeding however. So, after we had raised her haemoglobin to a safe level, we gave her an anaesthetic. I removed the blood-soaked pack and was able to find and stitch over the oozing edge of a laceration high in the vagina. The bleeding stopped. In all she received eight units of blood. She was out of the woods.

That's the thing about intensive care, it is brilliant at saving lives, particularly those of young people. It can get them over the life-threatening crisis and restore them to full health. When it comes to surviving severe medical nasties, you can't beat the resilience of youth – so often a life-saving factor in obstetric emergencies. When I started my training in the 1960s, we did not have intensive care units with ventilators and other technical wizardry – patients were 'specialled' in a side ward with one-to-one nursing care.

After two days in the ICU, we were able to transfer Mrs. Evans to our postnatal ward in the Women's Pavilion. She was soon cuddling and feeding her daughter and showing all the appropriate maternal qualities. Her baby had been transported with her and was looked after in our nursery while her mother was in ICU. Mr. Evans too, became more relaxed and secure with his wife's recovery. I saw them each day; they were not very chatty, and the controversial blood transfusion was never brought up. However, on the morning of her discharge she put her hand on my arm and said, "Thank you, Doctor, I know what everyone has done for me and I'm very grateful." Her husband added, "We both are."

So, that was it. I don't know if they were expelled from the church, but they did not seem resentful about the blood transfusion. I think Mr. Evans knew she would have died without it. I was satisfied that we had done the right thing – but then I would be, wouldn't I?

*

What about the ethics of all this? In the 1960s and 1970s medical ethics were just that – ethical principles guided by the medical and nursing professions. Medical decisions followed the, 'Do no harm' and, 'Do the right thing' maxims, along with basic decency and the, 'Do unto others as you would have them do unto you' principle. Rightly or wrongly, physicians were held in a position of trust and authority. This was exemplified by the annual litigation defence premium paid by physicians in Canada – one hundred dollars in 1970, versus tens of thousands of dollars in the 2000s. Informed consent and informed refusal were in place but not to the extent they are today. Doctors tended to consider all the options for treatment and present the patient with the plan he or she thought best. Nowadays, all the options are laid before the patient and they choose – which is a big improvement for patient autonomy.

By the 1980s a new profession of Biomedical Ethics emerged. The core of medical ethics was defined by four principles: beneficence (do good), non-maleficence (do no harm), autonomy (patient choice), and justice. This proved to be an employment bonanza for ethicists who became entrenched in hospital and university medical training programmes. They spoke a language that could only be completely understood by other ethicists – similar to the medical profession in that respect. Clinical conundrums were subject to lengthy discussion, sometimes with few definitive answers, often summarised by, "The doctor or nurse should do the best he or she can for the patient, after careful consideration of their unique individual circumstances etc. etc.….." Many of the more cynical senior doctors and nurses thought that's what they had been doing all along.

One area of clinical practice that changed significantly was a great increase in patient autonomy. The detailed information given to patients to provide informed consent was increased, and rightly so. Ethical principles were extended to guidelines published by the national licensing colleges, which, in essence, became the standard of care that all doctors were expected to follow. Part of these guidelines was the right of informed refusal – even of potentially life-saving treatment. This included the right of a woman to bleed to death in childbirth if she refused blood transfusion.

Decades after the above case I became aware of a similar clinical situation, although I was not involved. A young mother was allowed to bleed to death following delivery of her baby, when her right to refuse life-saving blood transfusion was respected.

So, early and late in my career I knew of two cases with contrasting outcomes, reflecting a changing ethical environment. One, managed with well-intentioned medical authoritarianism, resulting in a live mother. The other, managed with equally well-intentioned ethical respect for patient autonomy, and ending with a dead mother.

Chapter 36
Sister McCormick

It was a case of bilateral love at first sight. We two, Yvette McCormick and I, met on New Year's Eve 1958 and had our inaugural date in February 1959 – we have been going together ever since. Our first outing was to the Hippodrome Cinema in Belfast to see *Island in the Sun*, starring Harry Belafonte. I was in the middle of my first year of medical school, and Yvette was one month before starting as a student nurse at the Royal Victoria Hospital, Belfast. A description of some of the experiences of a student nurse in that era follows.

We have a copy of the *Rules for Student Nurses in Training* from the Royal Victoria Hospital, Belfast. This little booklet lists seventeen areas to which the rules apply. The first section, under the heading: *Age, Height, Education* etc. stated:

'They must be healthy, active and of good character. Not less that 5 feet 2 inches without shoes. Age between 18 and 30 years.'

Yvette met all these criteria except 'height' – at 5 feet, she was two inches short. She still disputes this but has never submitted to an independent measurement by any member of the family – nor have we encouraged this particular statistical evaluation.

A pre-training medical examination from her GP was a requirement, however. She told him she needed to be 5 feet 2 inches tall and, lo and behold, he measured her height at exactly that – first hurdle overcome. Application forms had, '…. to be completed in the Candidates own handwriting.' There was a four-month trial period.

The first eight weeks were done at The Beeches, a large house distant from the hospital, in which some twenty young women entered their Pre-Training School (PTS). They were to live in the Beeches Monday to Friday, had the weekend off, but were to return by ten p.m. Sunday. These ten p.m. curfews would be a constant throughout the three-year training period. One late pass to eleven p.m. was allowed per month, but it had to be requested directly from Matron or one of the Assistant Matrons. (As a result of the ten p.m. curfew we had to leave the cinema before the end of the movie on most of our evenings out – cinemas being one of the few places for couples to meet in Belfast at that time. Many years later our two sons would question why we were watching 'stupid old movies' on the television – we told them we wanted to see how they ended.)

During their time in the Beeches, they were taught the basics: proper bed making, with or without a patient in situ, giving bed baths, taking vital signs, chart recording, set-up of procedure trays, wound care, bandaging, first aid, etc. There were lectures on Anatomy and Physiology. Matron came and gave encouraging talks – emphasising the professional and ethical standards required of nurses. In one such talk she posed the question: "If you were a nurse in the First World War and had to look after two wounded soldiers, one British and one German, would you treat them differently?" The question was rhetorical and the answer was an emphatic 'no' – a patient is a patient, is a patient – and all are treated without judgement and to the best of your ability.

The students were measured for and received their uniforms – lots of starch was involved. This preparatory training ensured that when they started on the wards they would be of some use and wouldn't feel out of their depth.

The annual pay was £240 ($670.00), rising to £250 and £262 in the second and third years respectively. From this amount £113 was deducted for board and lodging. It worked out at just over £2 per week and, with the hours they worked, at about one shilling (5p) per hour. The rules booklet also contained a financially punitive warning under the heading, 'Duties':

'They may be required to pay half the cost of any article broken or damaged through carelessness or neglect.'

After eight weeks at the PTS, they moved to the nurse's residence at the RVH, and to their first duty on the wards. They were now proper 'Royal nurses.' Here their teacher and disciplinarian would be the ward sister. The chain of authority was very clear, and Sister's word was indisputable law. Student nurses had their own dining room. It was a bit like boarding school.

Nurses started on the wards at 7.45 a.m., had a breakfast break at about 9.30 a.m. and lunch at 1.30 p.m. They either worked 7.45 a.m. to 5 p.m. or had a break from 2 to 5 p.m. and returned to work until 8.30 p.m.

Each week they had one half day (work 7.45 a.m. to 1.30 p.m.) and one full day off. If the needs of the ward made it necessary, meal breaks could be missed and hours of duty extended – without question or dissent. Night duty started at 8.30 p.m. and went through to 8 a.m.

The student nurse training programme at the Royal was tightly structured and disciplined. There were study blocks of two to four weeks during which they were relieved of clinical duties and taught by Sister Tutors, with lectures, some given by medical staff, and with practical classes. There was continuous emphasis on professional appearance and comportment, punctuality, confidentiality and the highest standards of nursing care. From these consistent expectations a sense of camaraderie and pride emerged in the group. The majority of nursing care in the hospitals of Northern Ireland was provided by student nurses in training.

I have outlined much of the work done by nurses in preceding chapters. Take-in days and nights were always busy with the admission of all emergency cases for twenty-four hours. Every new admission had their hair fine-combed and inspected for head lice.

As the third-year student nurse in charge, Nurse McCormick remembers preparing five dead bodies in one night. This entailed washing the body, catheterising the bladder, tying up the jaw, bringing the feet together with a bandage, careful placement of the arms and of a sheet around the body – which was then collected by the mortuary attendant. After such a night, Nurse McCormick was criticised by Sister at the morning report, for having the audacity to call an extra nurse to help with the early morning injections. No recognition of a tough night or acknowledgement for coping with five deaths. Praise was not given, only criticism was on offer.

After such encounters the nurses would congregate in one of their bedrooms with cups of tea, and go over difficult cases and experiences. Stress and post-traumatic stress disorder were not in their vocabulary, but they instinctively knew the value of what would now be called group counselling. It was often carried out with near hysterical laughter mixed with tears – as noted in chapter thirteen.

Matron, or one of the Assistant Matrons visited each ward every day. Matron had quite a presence – it was almost like a royal visit. Sister, or the most senior nurse on duty, would accompany her on a quick walk around all of the beds in the ward. Matron would cast a critical eye on the tidiness of the ward in general and, in particular, on the standard of bed-making with the sheets carefully mitered at the corners. She would stop for an encouraging word with two or three of the patients. Her visit to each ward lasted only a few minutes, and one could criticise the superficial nature of this event. However, it was a throwback to the Florence Nightingale military era of nursing. In a sense, Matron was the commanding officer and her walk round let the nursing staff know she was keeping an eye on the front lines. For patients it was a reassuring reminder that the higher echelons of nursing were involved and interested in their welfare. It was all part of a single-minded commitment to the highest standards on the part of the senior nursing ranks – they were a special breed.

In other major hospitals in Belfast and in regional hospitals throughout the province similar standards were expected from their own nursing schools. Those of us who worked at the RVH, however, thought that you just couldn't beat a 'Royal-trained nurse.'

Nurse McCormick passed her exams, including awards for best practical nurse in two of her three student years, and in 1962 became Staff Nurse McCormick. Two years later she was elevated to a very young appointment as theatre (OR) Sister in Gynaecology. There was only one sister in each theatre, and it was as a senior red sister – a very big deal. I was still a medical student and now even further down the pecking order. In truth, theatre sisters tended to be younger and often did not remain in the position long.

In the 1960s a career as a senior nurse and marriage were mutually exclusive. This was brought home to Sister McCormick in 1965, when she chose to marry me – a very good decision, in my admittedly biased opinion. Nurses had to inform Matron when they were going to get married, and upon so doing Sister McCormick was told she could not be a full-time sister and a wife. This was just a statement of Matron's policy and not up for discussion. The senior consultant surgeons in gynaecology pleaded to have Sister McCormick remain in her post – to no avail, Matron had complete authority over the nursing staff. Matron made it clear that, despite being demoted back to Nurse McCormick, she was a valued member of the nursing staff and a suitable part time position would be made available.

So, that was it, demoted to part time Nurse McCormick for having the temerity to marry, and there was worse to come – she chose to be Nurse Baskett. All this at a time when we would have been glad of a full-time sister's salary. But there could be no argument, Matron rules, OK.

Sister Yvette McCormick - 1965

Bibliography

These articles and books provide background to some of the chapters in this book.

- Baskett TF, Carson RM. Paracervical block with bupivacaine. Canadian Medical Association Journal 1974; 110:1363-5.
- Baskett TF. Obstetric care in the central Canadian Arctic. British Medical Journal 1978; 2:1001-4.
- Baskett TF. A university department's involvement with medical care in the Canadian North. Canadian Medical Association Journal 1979; 120:298-300.
- Baskett TF. Maternity care in the north. University of Manitoba Medical Journal 1979; 49:24-7.
- Baskett TF, Baskett PJF. Frank Pantridge and mobile coronary care. Resuscitation 2001; 48:99-104.
- Baskett PJF, Baskett TF. Resuscitation Greats. Bristol: Clinical Press Ltd; 2007.
- Baskett TF. Essential Management of Obstetric Emergencies. Fifth Edition. Bristol: Clinical Press Ltd; 2015.
- Baskett TF, The Pill and the Pope. West of England Medical Journal 2016; 115:1-14.
- Baskett TF. A History of Caesarean Birth: From Maternal Death to Maternal Choice. Bristol: Clinical Press Ltd; 2017.
- Baskett TF. Eponyms and Names in Obstetrics and Gynaecology. Third Edition. Cambridge: Cambridge University Press; 2019.
- Clarke R. The Royal Victoria Hospital, Belfast: A History 1797-1997. Belfast: Blackstaff Press;1997.
- Cohen J, Baskett TF. Sterilization patterns in a Northern Canadian population. Canadian Journal of Public Health 1978; 69:222-4.
- Geddes JS, Stewart RD, Baskett TF. The Evolution of Pre-hospital Emergency Care. Bristol: Clinical Press Ltd; 2017.
- Gibson ED, Ritchie JWK, Armstrong MJ. The changing role of the obstetric flying squad. Ulster Medical Journal 1980; 49:126-130.
- Hogan C. Republic of Shame: How Ireland Punished 'Fallen Women' and Their Children. Dublin: Penguin Books; 2019.
- McAllister CM, Baskett TF. Female education and maternal mortality: a worldwide survey. Journal of Obstetrics and Gynaecology Canada 2006; 28:983-90.
- Moore S. The Irish on the Somme. Belfast: Local Press Ltd; 2005.
- Pantridge JF, Geddes JS. Cardiac arrest after myocardial infarction. Lancet 1966; 1:807-8
- Pantridge JF. An Unquiet Life: Memoirs of a Physician and Cardiologist. Antrim: Greystone Books; 1989.
- Payne D. Record number of Irish women visit Britain for abortion. British Medical Journal 1999; 319:593.
- Prince S, Warner G. Belfast and Derry in Revolt: A New History of the Start of the Troubles. Newbridge: Irish Academic Press; 2019.pp 38-52.